The Warrior-Scholar Ideal Revisited

New Essays on an Old Vision

Jack Kerwick, PH.D.
LtCol. Al Ridenhour, USMC (RET)

The Warrior-Scholar Ideal Revisited: New Essays on an Old Vision

Other books by Jack Kerwick

Misguided Guardians: The Conservative Case Against Neoconservatism
Christianity and the World: Essays Philosophical, Historical and Cultural
Higher Miseducation: A Dissident's Essays on the Assault against Liberal
Learning
The American Offensive: Dispatches from the Front

Cover Design by Guy D. Corp
www.GrafixCorp.com

STAIRWAY PRESS—APACHE JUNCTION

STAIRWAY≡PRESS

www.StairwayPress.com
1000 West Apache Trail
Suite 126
Apache Junction, AZ 85120 USA

Al Ridenhour

AL IS A retired U.S. Marine Corps Lieutenant Colonel with 28-years of service including multiple combat tours in Iraq and Afghanistan. He has held numerous command leadership positions including Weapons Company Executive Officer, Sniper Platoon Commander, Infantry Company Commander, Marine Intelligence Officer JTF-6 Counter Drug Mission, Intelligence Section Leader, Regimental Operations Officer, Anti-Terror Red Team Leader Iraq, Director of the Marine Corps lead agency to combat improvised explosive devices, Liaison and Marine Warfighting Lab Program Director Regional Command Southwest Afghanistan, and Marine Corps Liaison to the Joint Staff.

Upon retirement, he served as a Law Enforcement consultant to the NJ State Police Special Operations Section and

Regional Operations Intelligence Center, the FBI Philadelphia Bomb Section, and a subject matter expert to the US Department of Homeland Security's, Explosives Division.

Al is the CEO of Strength From Within, LLC; Creator and Founder of Warrior Flow Combatives and the President and Co-Founder of the International Warrior Arts Association (IWAA).

With over 40 years of Combative Arts experience, he is recognized as a self-defense expert worldwide and is highly sought out for seminars, workshops, lectures, and special individualized training.

He has lectured on terrorism at John Jay College of Criminal Justice, is the author of several books on self-defense and holds a BA in Criminal Justice and an MBA.

Jack Kerwick

JACK HOLDS A doctorate degree in philosophy from Temple University. He's been teaching philosophy at a number of American colleges and universities from the Southwest to the Northeast for over 25 years.

His work has appeared in scholarly journals, popular publications, anthologies and he is the author of four popular nonfiction books.

Kerwick is a black belt in Tang Soo Do, a certified Senior-Instructor in Warrior Flow Combatives and a member of the International Warrior Arts Association.

Recently, his work centers on revealing the inseparable connection between philosophy and the arts of war as resurrected in the Warrior-Scholar ideal.

Contents

INTRODUCTION 3

The Warrior-Scholar Ideal 3

ESSAY 1: 9

Why Train in a Martial Art? 9

ESSAY 2 15

Warrior Flow as an Art of War 15

ESSAY 3 26

The Truly Dangerous Man 26

ESSAY 4 31

Civilization and the Need to develop a Warrior Spirit...........31

ESSAY 5 35

Managing Fear...35

ESSAY 6 38

Lessons from Childhood for Politics: Fear and Bullying.........38

ESSAY 7 42

This Thing Called "Fear" 42

ESSAY 8 47

The Need for "Ruthless Intent" 47

ESSAY 9 52

Thoughts on Guns, Violence, and Self-Protection...............52

ESSAY 11 57

Rising Crime, Self-Protection, and Finding Honest Martial
Instruction 57

ESSAY 12 66

More on Ruthless Intent...66

ESSAY 13 71

Ruthless Intent: It's Cultivation..................................71

ESSAY 14 76

On Manhood: The Warrior Part I......................................76

ESSAY 15 81

Guns and Self-Protection: Lessons from the Uvalde Shooting and
its Political Aftermath...81

ESSAY 16 87

Tips for Combat-Readiness in a Hostile Political Environment 87

ESSAY 17 92

Martial Arts and Critical Thinking.................................92

ESSAY 18 97

Martial Arts and Paradigms 97
ESSAY 19 103
Self-Protection and the Problem of Fetishizing "Techniques" 103
ESSAY 20 108
On an Art of War 108
ESSAY 21 117
Transforming into a Warrior 117
ESSAY 22 123
Focusing on What Matters in the Warrior Arts 123
ESSAY 23 128
Warrior Flow 9 128
ESSAY 24 135
The Use of Evil Exemplars in Martial Training................. 135
ESSAY 25 140
Reminders to Warriors and Bad Guys 140
ESSAY 26 145
The Principles of Warrior Flow 145
ESSAY 27 151
The Metaphysics and Philosophy of Knowledge of Warrior Flow
.... 151
ESSAY 28 158
Self-Protection Begins at Home 158
ESSAY 29 162
The CATEGORICAL IMPERATIVES of the Warrior…and of
Warrior Flow 162
ESSAY 30 166
Keeping Combat Impersonal 166
ESSAY 31 171
The Enemy, not My Enemy: Setting the Mind for Victory in
Battle 171
ESSAY 32 177
Rory Miller's *Meditations on Violence: A Comparison of Martial Arts
Training & Real World Violence*: A Review 177

INTRODUCTION

The Warrior-Scholar Ideal

ALL OF THE WORLD'S wisdom traditions have always distinguished reality from mere appearance. All have some conception of enlightenment, some account of the painful, but liberating, odyssey from the illusions of the masses to the order of being, the realm of Truth and Light reached by only the few.

And it is reached by only the few precisely because the pursuit of truth is indeed *painful*. It comes at a cost, the cost of *alienation*. The pursuer of truth can expect to experience a sense of alienation from the masses, and even from among those with whom he had been close, because the pursuit tends to terminate in conclusions that are radically at odds with whatever the conventional wisdom happens to be at any given moment.

Pursuers of the truth, in other words, are fundamentally misguided if they think that their pursuit will make them popular with the majority. It will not. It may make them infamous, but it will not make them popular, for the heterodox aren't known to elicit the admiration of the orthodox. Dissidents tend not to endear themselves to the conformists whose worldview they're busy dismantling.

Arrogance, self-delusion, willful ignorance, intellectual flaccidity, an impoverished imagination, moral exhibitionism, and, critically, a conspicuous lack of courage—these are the character deficiencies that, in varying degrees and combinations, are nowhere in more ample supply than among the academics, journalists, pundits, comprehensively, the intellectual class of contemporary Western societies.

While the reasons for this are many, it is our thesis that, to no small extent, a pernicious, if largely inchoate, metaphysic of the human person accounts for the current situation. Although many intellectuals (and pseudo-intellectuals), if they aren't outright hostile to traditional forms of theism, are at the very least secular in their outlook, it nevertheless remains the case that implicit in our political-cultural institutions, particularly among the intelligentsia, is a mind-body dualism that continues to operate as the dominant default presupposition.

And it is this separation of the mental from the physical that explains why contemporary societies, especially Western societies, have long ago abandoned an ideal that was endorsed by cultures around the world and throughout the ages.

This rejected ideal is that of the Warrior-Scholar.

The prevailing worldview, the political-moral Zeitgeist of the West, is, essentially, a skyscraper of *lies*, of delusions that serve at once the material interests of the various elite classes that promote them and the psychological needs of the masses who uncritically imbibe them. Yet just as any literal skyscraper ensures that those who occupy its heights are far removed from the ground, so too does this great skyscraper of lies ensure that those who endorse it remain far removed from the ground of reality.

We submit that it was this single realization—the realization that the ruling classes rule by the Lie and the ruled are only and always too eager to obey the Lie—that gave rise to the ideal of the *Warrior-Scholar:*

> *The society that separates its scholars from its warriors*
> *will have its thinking done by cowards and its fighting*
> *done by fools.*

This quotation is widely attributed to Thucydides, an ancient Greek distinguished for having authored *The History of the Peloponnesian War*—a war in which he himself participated as a general. Yet whether Thucydides actually made this remark is neither here nor there. The point that it embodies expresses the consensus of the ages. The Japanese Samurai Miyamoto Musashi underscored this idea in his own way in the 17th century:

> *It is said the warrior's is the twofold Way of Pen and*
> *Sword, and he should have a taste for both Ways.*

Our society, regrettably, but unsurprisingly, has indeed betrayed the wisdom of the race by severing the pen from the sword, the scholar from the warrior, the mind from the body. Accordingly, we have suffered the consequences, as the vast majority of intellectuals, even when—*especially* when—they are self-styled "subversives," can be counted upon to deploy their resources to the end of *legitimizing* the reigning ideological rationalization of the ruling class.

Intellectuals, having betrayed their historical calling, are now herd animals, joint-enterprisers whose shared end it is to reinforce the prejudices of the *Regime*, the constellation of "regimes of power," as the postmodern philosopher Michel Foucault referred to the cultural institutions, formal and informal, that serve the interests of the State.

Government, academia, the media, the entertainment and tech industries, corporate America, and even the world of professional sports constitute a unified Regime inasmuch as they are alike purveyors of a single ruling ideology, a single political orthodoxy. Intellectuals, with all too few exceptions, supply the philosophical underpinnings, the abstract fantasies, for that ideology. In glaring contrast to Socrates, who, having paid the ultimate price for his labors, correctly saw himself as a "gad fly" to his society, today's intellectuals are the lapdogs of those same powers. They are apologists for the status quo.

It is our thesis that the current situation stands a chance of being remedied by way of a resurrection of the Warrior-Scholar ideal.

To put it bluntly, training in a martial art—a *genuine* martial art, an art of *war*—promises to go a long way toward restoring the intellectual to his—or *her*—proper place. This will require some unpacking, but suffice it to say for now that we are emphatically not saying that intellectuals must join the military in order to redeem themselves. The military, being a governmental institution, is not only of a piece with the very Regime that it is the calling of the intellectual to challenge; the military is this Regime's principal apparatus of power. As such, far too frequently, and for considerations that have little to nothing to do with keeping the citizens of its country safe, soldiers are deployed to kill and die.

What we are contending is that intellectuals should train in an art for the purpose of acquiring the skill and the will to protect themselves and other innocents from bodily harm, an art designed to instill in them the ability and the determination—the ruthless intention—to extinguish the life from the predatory thugs who would be reckless enough, stupid enough, to target them.

And if, for whatever reasons, the decent die in the course of protecting themselves and their own, then the art in which they invested their resources in training should be one that prepares them to embrace their fate, and to die with honor, with dignity.

Intellectuals need to train their bodies so that they can better train their minds. Training their bodies means subjecting them to trauma. More precisely, it means subjecting them to being struck, battered even, and battered to the point at which they are made to feel that unless they move and give as good as they're getting, they're never going to be more than the proverbial inch away from losing their lives. With a competent instructor in a warrior art, this will be the training modality to which they'll become accustomed.

In hardening the body and acquiring more physical courage, intellectuals stand a greater chance in turn of growing in mental courage—a virtue conspicuous for its absence among their number. Physical training, training in a warrior art, can only strengthen the intellectual's resolve to, at long last, observe Kant's imperative, *"Sapere aude!"* For Kant, this piece of Latin sums up the whole of the Enlightenment, for it means, *"Dare to know,"* or "Dare to *think*."

Of course, it isn't just intellectuals for whom these essays are written. The Warrior-Scholar ideal, a lost ideal, can be realized by anyone who is willing to endeavor toward it.

And we are convinced that it *should* be an ideal toward which more people strive.

The quality of public discourse generally can only be improved by decent people, from whatever background, achieving the discipline that can only be achieved through training in a real martial art. Contemporary politics, after all, are underwritten by fear. It isn't just that the fortunes of partisans among the political and media classes depend upon their constituents being forever in a state of anxiety, though this is demonstrably the case. In addition, though, it's also true—though it's seldom spoken of in "polite company," and largely goes unnoticed by most people—that there is a visceral, if subliminal, fear that accounts for why people vote as they do and make the public pronouncements that they make. Fear of "Cancel Culture," fear of being branded as a "racist" or "transphobe," or, yes, fear of being physically attacked by a mob hell-bent upon advancing the cause of "anti-fascism" or something along these lines—fear is the fuel that powers the engine of our politics.

But martial training, when it is an education in a genuine art of war, empowers students by enabling them to surmount their fears, and it does *this* by equipping them with the practical wisdom to discern when their fears are rational and when, as is overwhelmingly the case, they are not.

We're willing to go so far as to say that by resurrecting the Warrior-Scholar ideal, by reimagining for our day and age possibilities for self-actualization that had been taken for granted in most places for much of human history, we can come that much closer to realizing a politics of "emancipation."

Yet politics isn't really our primary concern at this time. *Self*-empowerment is our focus.

The essays that follow had been written over a period of the last three years, and can be read in any order. In the spirit of rote learning, themes recur, for the intention of compiling them into a book is to introduce and cultivate in readers a warrior state of mind. To this end, readers will be familiarized with Warrior Flow Combatives, the martial system of which Al is the founder and in which Jack is a Senior-Instructor.

One final note: While the following essays enclosed here are indeed written from the perspective of our art, one needn't be a practitioner or even an aspiring practitioner of Warrior Flow in order to acquire the psyche, a warrior consciousness, that this book is designed to shape.

It is our hope that readers find the vision laid out in these pages as edifying as it is unconventional.

ESSAY 1:

Why Train in a Martial Art?

TO THIS QUESTION, answers of several different types have been supplied. Typically, people claim that it is for the purpose of *self-defense* that they selected a martial art within which to train. While there are other benefits, like overall health and fitness, to be gotten from regular training in a martial art, it is typically self-defense first and foremost that people claim they want to learn.

To determine the meaningfulness of this answer, though, we need to be clear as to the meaning of "self-defense."

For that matter, we must as well determine the meaning of "martial art."

In contemporary commercialized societies like, say, the United States, martial arts have largely (even if not solely) come to be identified with *sports*. Within this model of **Martial Arts as Sport (MAS)**, self-defense is assumed to consist of skills that will enable students to win a duel, i.e. the proverbial mano-a-mano transaction of the kind that features in the ring or dojo.

That former Navy Seal and popular podcaster Jocko Willink subscribes to this paradigm became obvious when Willink said that unless people train in "boxing, Muay Thai, wrestling, or BJJ," they can't learn how to "fight."

The truth of the matter, though, is that the martial artists of bygone times and places wouldn't have been able to make heads or tails of this way of conceiving matters. Historically and etymologically, "martial" means "of or pertaining to war." Martial artists were students of the arts of *war*, and martial artists trained to become *warriors*.

They trained, that is, to become efficient, brutal, killing machines.

While, in some instances, there was an air of sport in the kinds of duels to which, say, Miyamoto Musashi went across the countryside challenging Japan's more reputable swordsmen, this was only an air, for the duels in which samurais and other swordsmen fought were duels to *the death*. There were no referees, no weight classes, no battery of restrictions designed to preclude participants from seriously injuring, to say nothing of killing, one another.

Musashi, let us not forget, was but 13 years of age when he won his first duel. A samurai known as Arima Kihei posted a challenge to battle all comers. Musashi signed his name to it. Musashi was in the custody of his uncle, Dorin, and a messenger arrived at Dorin's home to inform him that Kihei accepted the duel with his nephew.

Shocked and scared, Dorin pleaded with Kihei to call it off. Kihei replied that to preserve his honor, he would consent to spare the adolescent Musashi, but only if the latter would apologize to him at the time that the duel was scheduled to proceed.

At this moment, it was Dorin who began to apologize repeatedly and profusely for his nephew's impulsiveness. As he was doing so, Musashi charged at Kihei with a six-foot quarterstaff [a pole weapon], while Kihei in turn went at Musashi with a

10

wakizashi [a sword worn at one's side]. It was the kid, though, who had the upper hand, for he slammed Kihei to the ground, split him between the eyes, and bludgeoned him to death.

At *13 years of age*, Musashi was already shaping up to become one hell of a martial artist. Yet, forgiving the anachronisms, he succeeded in doing this in the absence of training in boxing, wrestling, Muay Thai, and Brazilian Jiu Jitsu.

He didn't assume a conventional boxing stance and square off with Arima Kihei. He wasn't interested in exchanging fists with him while bobbing and weaving. Nor did he care about going to the ground with Kihei and grappling. He was concerned only with destroying Kihei as quickly as possible.

And *this* is an entirely different mindset than that which is cultivated by athletes who equate the martial arts with sports.

Musashi, in glaring contrast, epitomizes another paradigm: **Martial Arts as War (MAW).** ("MAW" may be meaningless by reason of redundancy, for as was mentioned above, both etymologically and, in practice, historically, "martial" means "of or pertaining to war.")

Replete are stories of peerless athletes, professional fighters of various sorts, having their worldviews subverted in various ways in violent confrontations outside of a sport venue. One particularly telling incident involved Anthony Smith, a UFC light heavyweight fighter who ranks fifth in the world. Smith is also a black belt in BJJ.

Smith was asleep in his Nebraska home with his wife, kids, and mother-in-law two years ago when he was awakened by an intruder, Luke Haberman. Smith, at 6'4" and well over 200 pounds, had much in the way of size and strength over the 5'7", 170-pound Haberman. And yet Smith remarked that his confrontation with Haberman had been "one of the toughest" and most "terrifying" of his life.

"No normal human is able to fight like that," Smith said. "I'm by no means the baddest dude on the planet. But he's a regular Joe and I had a hard time dealing with him. And he took everything that I gave him—every punch, every knee, every elbow. He took every single one of them and kept fighting me."

It wasn't until the police arrived that Haberman would be subdued by Smith and two officers.

Smith is to be commended for having defended his family. However, there can be no question that one central reason that accounts for why the melee lasted for as long as it did (about five minutes or so—an eternity in a real, life-or-death battle) is that Smith, caught unawares, defaulted to his training, training designed to prevail over opponents in a cage.

Undoubtedly, another reason that no one was killed is that the intruder, Haberman, was a high school wrestling champion. At 20, he had been out of school only a few years. It's more than a little probable that *his* training preempted him from possessing the kind of murderous intention that may have otherwise been present.

In short, neither Smith nor Haberman were trying to kill one another, for neither had ever trained to kill. This isn't to say that things couldn't have eventuated in someone's death. It's only to note that the violence that unfolded between them was more on the order of a match, however brutal, than a state of war, for neither ever conditioned themselves for war.

Popular podcaster Joe Rogan, himself a former MMA fighter, expressed incredulity toward his guest, another former professional MMA competitor, Brendan Schaub, that Smith, who he described as "one of the baddest motherf**kers walking the Earth," "didn't...just choke" Haberman "unconscious." After all, Rogan reasoned, the intruder was "smaller than" Smith and yet "he took everything that" Smith "could throw at him." Schaub concurred by asking: "Why didn't he [Smith] just choke the f—k out of him?"

That the dynamic that transpired between Smith and Haberman was of a fundamentally different kind than any that Rogan and Schaub ever experienced between themselves and their opponents in a ring is a brute fact that, it's painfully obvious, is lost upon them.

Being abruptly awaken in the middle of the night, in the dark, by a total stranger who you have every reason to believe means you and yours harm is a condition that is as far from those conditions under which sports fighters perform than Heaven is from Hell. If Rogan and Schaub had the slightest appreciation of this, they wouldn't have asked the question that they asked. They would have asked *not* why a family man, the protector of his family and home, didn't "choke *out*" a violent home intruder. They would've asked why he didn't choke *to death* that intruder.

Or they would've questioned why he didn't grab a lamp or some other makeshift weapon and bludgeon the violent intruder until he was satisfied that the intruder was neutralized, or why Smith (reportedly) waited until his mother-in-law handed him a knife before he thought to grab one himself to filet the thug who threatened him and his loved ones.

The point is this: sport or contest fighting is all well and good. But the training, both mental and physical, appropriate to it is not only different from that suited for war. The two are incompatible in critical, essential respects.

Outside of sports, the only violence for which a person should prepare him or herself is potentially mortal violence, the violence of war. And the only justification for using violence is defense of oneself and innocents against imminent, life-endangering aggression.

This in turn means that *if* a person must fight as the only alternative to being victimized, then, in principle, it is, and can only be, a fight to the finish.

That is, the person who trains for real self-defense must train so as to make him or herself as capable and willing as possible to die and kill, for while it's possible that the incapacitation of an attacker (or attackers) won't require anyone to lose their lives, the resolve to go to that place must exist in advance of the confrontation. A defender may determine that the neutralization of the attacker doesn't require lethal measures. If not, the defender can dial things back. If so, the defender can do what he or she needs to do.

In other words, the essential point of training in a martial art, an art of war, is to become a warrior, to protect oneself and one's own, by whichever means necessary, from predators.

To train in a martial art is, fundamentally, to train so as to acquire the will and the skill to annihilate the violent who would prey upon innocents.

ESSAY 2

Warrior Flow as an Art of War

AS WE'VE NOTED before, far too many self-defense instructors within the world of the martial arts ignore the contextual considerations that inform every training modality.

There is, however, one system that recognizes that—to paraphrase Pindar, the lyric poet quoted by the ancient Greek historian Herodotus—*context is king*.

The system to which we refer—and it *is* a genuine *system*, as opposed to being of a piece with the ad hoc assemblage of techniques that passes for many a self-defense school—is Warrior Flow Combatives.

Founded by retired USMC Lieutenant-Colonel Al Ridenhour, Warrior Flow is as real a "reality-based" system of self-defense as any that exists.

Below, we elaborate on the remarks regarding Warrior Flow that have been made elsewhere.

So as to avoid confusion, the original comments are in in

15

bold-faced type:

1. *Most fundamentally, the martial art instructor must be ever-mindful that "martial" means "of or pertaining to war." Quite literally, the martial arts are nothing more or less than the warrior arts, the arts of war.*

    And martial artists are, literally, those who train for war.

"*Warrior* Flow" is called such for a reason. To be certain, the term "warrior" is wielded, not just liberally, but downright profligately these days. All who survive a disease, advance a political cause, exercise hard, or pray regularly are regarded (either by themselves or others) as "warriors." While such folks may very well be good and just human beings, their accomplishments do not make them warriors.

Yet Ridenhour, veteran of multiple tours of duty and many combat operations, knows that a genuine martial art is indeed a warrior art, for the martial arts were fashioned for the purpose of achieving victory in war.

Those who assume the study of a martial art, then, and whether they realize it consciously or not, have committed to train to become warriors. If this point is not clear to them initially, it is the responsibility of their prospective instructors to spare not a moment in making it so.

It is up to their prospective instructors, in other words, to clarify to them that, like soldiers training for victory in war over the enemy on the battlefield, so too must anyone who decides to train under them train always with an eye toward settling for nothing less than victory in war over the enemy that they may one day encounter on the streets, in their homes, or anywhere else.

Martial arts students, those who train for what is commonly known as "self-defense," must train for war. They must train to become, literally, warriors.

2.   *Since those who seek out self-defense instructors do so in*
     The Warrior-Scholar Ideal Revisited in order to become
     as proficient as they can in the art of decimating
     assailants who threaten them and their own, this entails
     that their instructors know the difference between so-
     called "combat" sports, on the one hand, and, on the
     other, the nature of war, or what is typically known as
     "reality-based self-defense.

Incredibly, many a self-defense instructor do not appear to recognize that sport fighting and potentially mortal combat, or "self-defense," are different languages. Much less do they recognize the mutual *incommensurability* of these two languages, for it is in fact true that the terms of the one can't even be translated into those of the other: There is no common denominator or standard by which they can be evaluated.

Consider it like this:

What is commonly called a "self-defense" or "combatives system" presupposes, or should presuppose, a certain *paradigm*. This paradigm I have elsewhere referred to as "MAW"—**Martial Arts as War**.

In glaring contrast, classical martial arts systems (in their contemporary, commercialized form), boxing, MMA, Brazilian Jiu-Jitsu, etc. presuppose an altogether different paradigm: "MAS"—**Martial Arts as Sport**.

Thomas Kuhn, who himself had a Ph.D. in physics, became unquestionably one of the 20th century's most prominent philosophers of science. His landmark book, *The Structure of Scientific Revolutions,* upended the traditional view of science as a progressively-accumulating, value-neutral body of knowledge that scientists dispassionately piece together by building upon the work of their predecessors. This is fiction. It is a myth, Kuhn argued. The truth is that science always transpires within a paradigm, or a "disciplinary matrix:" a community or Gestalt of shared assumptions, concerns, interests, and values.

Paradigms are stable until and unless they are beset by "crises," problems that the paradigm lacks sufficient resources to resolve. If and when the crisis becomes insurmountable, the paradigm implodes and eventually becomes replaced by a new one altogether.

Paradigms are incommensurable because there is no standard that they share in common.

MAW and MAS are paradigms or disciplinary matrixes. That a punch is but a punch and a kick but a kick, to paraphrase Bruce Lee, can seductively delude us into thinking that they are but different dialects of the same language. They are nothing of the kind. The assumptions, concerns, interests, and values of the one and those of the other are mutually antithetical.

Warrior Flow instructors are well aware of this. They are well aware that their system operates within the paradigm of MAW. Thus, its training modalities and methodologies are designed accordingly.

More precisely, the essential training modality of Warrior Flow is predicated upon the presupposition that the Enemy—anyone and everyone who would prey upon innocents—is invariably bigger, stronger, faster, more athletic, and more ruthless than the Warrior Flow student. While on its face this may at first glance appear self-defeating, there is a method to the madness:

On the basis of this postulate, the student trains tirelessly to move as *efficiently* as possible in *his or her own body*—a person's unique body, with all of its idiosyncrasies, its age and history of vulnerabilities, of injuries—so as to be able to neutralize all of these physical advantages of the Enemy.

To summarily put it in perspective, a woman in her 60s or 70s may not fare too well in a cage fight against a MMA athlete in *his* 20s. However, as for her odds of being able to move her body just enough—just *well* enough—to stab the same kind of guy in his throat in the event that he aggresses against her on the street or in her home? Well, they are far greater in *the absence of any training* as long as she has the determination to survive the attack.

With Warrior Flow training, she has that much more of an advantage, for her training will equip her with the skill and the will, the "*ruthless intention*," to not just *survive*, but to achieve *victory* over the Enemy.

3. *The average person who pursues self-defense is not a 20-something year old male athlete in prime physical condition. Aspiring self-defense students are typically middle aged (and older), and they include men and women who are only interested in learning to train in a way that will enable them to move so as to compensate for whatever aches, pains, and injuries they've acquired over their lifetimes. No small number of those who enroll for self-defense training may have otherwise been living relatively sedentary lifestyles for decades before they enroll.*

   It's not just that they aren't especially athletic, and perhaps were never so. Neither are they bouncers, bodyguards, corrections officers, police officers, and military personnel.

   Some may have never been in a fist fight. They may have never thrown a strike. Some may have never picked up a weight.

To judge from the training methodologies of many self-defense systems, one could be forgiven for thinking that the world of reality-based self-defense is ridden with a virtually systemic ignorance of the profile of the average self-defense student!

There are some techniques that a reasonably fit guy in his 20s or early 30s who is manning the door of a nightclub, guarding prisoners, or making arrests on the streets could, because of both the context within which he is operating as well as the physical assets that he already possesses, may very well make work. These same techniques, however, become infeasible, even unintelligible, when taught to civilians who don't fit this profile.

For example, Geoff Thompson, a world-renowned combatives instructor, teaches what has become known as the "two-touch" rule. Lee Morrison, a comparably elite instructor, teaches his students the same. The idea here is that if an aggressor invades your space and touches you, you give him a pass on that one as you're moving slightly back with your arm extended to create space between the two of you as you continue to assure him that you don't want any trouble. But if he comes in to touch you a *second* time, then you are to unload on him.

Thompson and Morrison both worked "the doors" of some of London's notoriously seedy clubs. As bouncers or "*doormen*," and *young* bouncers at that, something like this "two-touch" rule made a lot of sense.

For middle-aged or older citizens who are only interested in defending themselves and their families against violent attack by predators, the two-touch rule is unduly risky, possibly reckless.

In fact, it conveys, *at best,* a mixed message, for if civilian self-defense training is supposed to equip people with the skill and the will to use violence only for the purpose of genuine self-protection—if, in other words, students are taught to employ their new powers only when it is absolutely necessary to do so, when they believe that they're lives are potentially threatened—then their training should encapsulate, as Warrior Flow training encapsulates, what we may call the "*no touch*" rule.

In principle, if it's possible for a belligerent to touch you, then it's possible for him to kill you. Thus, the moment the aggressor, with an hostility of intention that is intuitively discernible, starts to move into a defender's space, his or her "sphere of influence," as it's referred to as in Warrior Flow, the defender's training would have predisposed him or her to preempt the attack by besieging the attacker with strikes meant to, at a minimum, send the attacker on a trip to the intensive care unit. If the cause of self-defense demands a one way visit to the morgue for the attacker, so be it.

To repeat, a martial art is such in name only unless and until it endows students with the ability and the resolve to achieve victory in war. A self-defense system is one in name only until and unless it equips students with the skill and the will to annihilate those who jeopardize their lives and/or the lives of the innocents in their charge.

On this point, there can be no ambiguity.

An encounter that one has good reason to believe could be but seconds away from materializing into a violent attack is not a game or a ritual of some sort. It is *war*. Nor is war merely a metaphor for such an assault. The sort of violence for which reality-based self-defense instructors prepare their students, and the sort of violence for which self-defense students seek to prepare themselves, is what is typically called "asocial" or "anti-social" violence, an attack on one's person or one's own by a perfect stranger. It can be every bit as deadly as any violent exchange on the battlefield.

Asocial violence is predatory in nature.

Asocial violence is contrasted with "social" violence, i.e. proverbial "fights" that had escalated by way of a previous exchange of some sort and that, as such, can almost always be diffused beforehand.

For this reason, there can be no dicking around. Warrior Flow instruction cultivates in its students a triadic mindset. Its three components are: Perfect Clarity, Moral Certainty, and Ruthless Intention.

Perfect Clarity: Once a belligerent violates the imaginary trip wire in their minds by invading their space, Warrior Flow practitioners know exactly the course of action—total warfare— that they must take. There is no ambiguity.

Moral Certainty: Warrior Flow practitioners know beyond any possibility of a doubt that they have the moral right and the duty to wage total warfare upon anyone who threatens their lives and those of other innocents within their orbit. They are convicted of the righteousness of their cause, for no one else has

21

the right to harm them or theirs. War is not, as some would have us think, beyond all moral considerations. War, like self-defense, is a preeminently ethical enterprise. The waging of war may be just or unjust. Warrior Flow students know that if they have to wield the sword, so to speak, then their cause must be righteous, and that it is always righteous to pursue victory over those who pose imminent danger to the innocent.

Ruthless Intention: Warrior Flow students train so as to be able, at the proverbial flip of the switch, to attack assailants with unadulterated ruthlessness. This is the will to, not take one's chances trying to disarm, restrain, or otherwise force an attacker into submission but, rather, incapacitate him by whichever means necessary, with ruthless efficiency.

4. *Knowing their students means knowing that the average person who pursues self-defense training does so because they harbor fears generally and, specifically, the fear that they lack what it takes to rise to the task of defending themselves and their loved ones if the need to do so ever arises.*

Warrior Flow instructors eschew the language of "survival" in favor of "victory." Survival is bare existence. Victory, however, connotes a moral achievement. In doing so, it reinforces the Warrior Flow student's conviction that self-defense is indeed an ethical imperative.

As for the scary stories with which self-defense instructors reinforce the fears of their students, Warrior Flow instructors are having none of them. They know, and respect, their students—who, as I've noted in my last article, are the last people on the planet who need to be reminded that they shouldn't go around looking to brawl with outlaw bikers, gangbangers, mobsters, and other varieties of criminal low lives. Self-defense students tend to be the last people who need to be incessantly reminded of the need to avoid potentially violent encounters with *anyone*.

Yet it isn't just that Warrior Flow instructors don't immortalize the bad guys. They emphatically underscore the bad guys' *mortality*. No matter who they are or who they know, no matter how "tough" or rough they may be, the bad guys, whether they are alone or in a group—yes, Warrior Flow students train so as to eliminate multiple attackers, if need be—are vulnerable to being injured, maimed, and killed like anyone and everyone else.

Bad guys *are* scary, for sure. The objective that Warrior Flow sets for its students is that of making *the bad guys scared,* and scared of *them.* The bad guys learn to become aggressive and ruthless. Warrior Flow instructors believe that if the wicked can learn to acquire these traits, so too can the decent who train for self-defense. Only in the case of the decent, the aggressiveness and ruthlessness that they cultivate will be reserved only for the scumbags who prey upon innocents.

Regarding the warning about the possibility of self-defense students getting arrested in the event that they defend themselves, this too can, if issued frequently enough, impede students from defending themselves if and when they need to do so, for the fear of legal repercussions—a fear that many already had prior to enrolling in a self-defense system—could lodge in their psyches.

To repeat: The average self-defense student no more needs to be instructed to fear getting arrested than he or she needs to be instructed to fear mixing it up with evil doers. It's precisely this fear that brought him or her to enroll in self-defense.

What self-defense instructors are obligated to offer their students is training that will help them surmount these fears by managing them.

And they can supply *this* service by teaching students how to put foot to ass if and when they must.

They can supply it by being, well, self-defense instructors.

Warrior Flow instructors aspire to do just this. They don't go on about the need for their students to avoid bad guys because bad guys are bad and because, if students harm the bad guys, they may get arrested. Students know this.

(Warrior Flow instructors do, however, implore students to refrain from talking to the police until they have legal representation—even if they are absolutely certain that their use of violence was unequivocally an instance of legitimate self-defense. Under duress and in the heat of the moment, it's possible for a person to speak inaccurately or otherwise in ways that could, potentially, be self-incriminatory.)

5. Finally, many self-defense instructors issue advice to their students that they themselves never admit to having followed themselves.

Usually, martial arts, self-defense experts tell their students to run if confronted with danger. To this counsel we take no objection—as long as it is *framed within context*, which it scarcely ever is. Warrior Flow instructors train their students to avail themselves of a tactical retreat *if and when this is a possibility*. Yet they never issue running as a categorical prescription. Many would-be victims *can't* run, and even those who are sufficiently mobile to move with relative speed may intuit that running from a determined attacker may be futile, or may provide the attacker with more time and opportunity that he wouldn't have had otherwise to successfully execute his designs.

At bottom, students are not investing their resources in time, energy, trust, and money in martial instruction in order to be told to *run* if and when confronted by aggressors. Chances are good that running, whether literally or mentally, is an activity with which self-defense students have had a lifetime to become acquainted. It's because they want to be able to avail themselves of another option that they decided to take up the study of self-defense in the first place.

They didn't pursue self-defense for their instructors to turn around and tell them to continue doing what they have already been doing.

Warrior Flow instructors take their vocation, and their students' sense of self, seriously. They train students, to the best of their ability, to be able to crucify those who would aggress against them and theirs.

Warrior Flow instructors try to make their students not only every bit as good as themselves but, if possible, even *better*.

ESSAY 3

The Truly Dangerous Man

OUR WORK ON the obligations of martial arts instructors have elicited several responses. We won't bother addressing all of them. We will, however, clear up some confusion.

First, we have never said that a person in a potentially dangerous situation should *never* run. Of course, there is such a thing as a tactical retreat. Rather, we criticized those instructors who, *indiscriminately* and *categorically*, i.e. without any regard for the circumstances of the attacker or attackers and those of the person under attack, tell their students to *run*. This is stupid and perilous advice if the prospective victim *can't run*. For an elderly person, or a person who is not elderly but who has sustained injuries that render running a sub-optimal course of action, this advice, if followed, could very well make the attacked person that much more vulnerable.

Or maybe a person could run, all things being equal. Running may still not be the way to go, for it buys the attacker

26

the *time* he needs to give chase. It could increase his odds of successfully executing his attack.

So, to be clear, we never stated that a person should never run. And this means that we never said that he or she should always "*fight.*"

For that matter, strictly speaking, we never urged anyone to *fight*—ever. There's a reason for this:

Athletes in competition with one another "fight." And that is all fine and good. Adolescents, and those adolescents who never cease being such even long after they've come to inhabit adult bodies, "fight." When the former fight, while it is generally to be discouraged, it is expected and regarded as a part of maturing. When the latter fight, it's pathetic.

Those who enroll in a martial art for the purpose of self-protection train to *kill.* They train to become dangerous, but a danger to would-be assailants.

In other words, a serious student of the martial arts does not engage in the sorts of "street fights" and "bar brawls" for which far too many YouTube martial arts instructors appear all too eager to prepare the viewers of their channels. A student who trains in a martial art should be training, not to fight, but to wage *war*, and to do so for no other purpose than that of *victory* (and not mere "*survival*").

But if one is to wage war, then one is to unleash unremitting violence only in the event that one is imminently threatened and there are no other options. And what *this* in turn means is that the student of a martial art will not think to waste his time engaging some shit-talking, chest-thumping, dick-swinging moron. The stuff that can be avoided, will be avoided, and this kind of stuff is all stuff that is readily avoidable.

In 1986, Charlie Reese, a writer for *The Orlando Sentinel*, charged Ronald Reagan, "a nice man," with failing to "understand the world, which is just as barbaric as ever." What concerns us is not the accuracy or not of Reese's critique of Reagan. Rather, it is his analysis of "the truly dangerous man," and how the truly dangerous man differs from the proverbial "tough guy," the obnoxious asshole with whom far too many martial artists seem to be preoccupied.

Reese's description couldn't be more on point:

> The truly dangerous man does not wear camouflage fatigues or muscle shirts. He does not talk loudly, boast how tough he is, give demonstrations or make threats. The truly dangerous man dresses inconspicuously and is soft- spoken. He walks away from most confrontations. The only time you learn that the truly dangerous man is mad at you is a split second before you die, for he never fights. He only kills. The truly dangerous man knows that fighting is what children do and killing is what men do.

Those Americans who train to become truly dangerous men—or *women*—train to exercise their Second Amendment right, for what both gun enthusiasts and gun-controllers seem to miss is that while the right to "bear *arms*" does indeed affirm the right to use guns for purposes of protection, the latter implies the more fundamental right to self-protection *by whatever means*.

The Second Amendment, then, codifies a *martial* spirit that its Framers expected would be diffused among the free citizens for whom it was meant.

The conventional wisdom, shared by gun enthusiasts and gun grabbers alike, would have us think that the gun was on the order of a magic wand, an effortless substitute for martial training. The gun is indeed, *potentially*, a great equalizer. But it is only as good as the person who wields it. If the gun-bearer, however great a shot he may be on the range while shooting at stationary targets, isn't sufficiently quick to get the jump on the bad guy, or if he doesn't train to shoot, under the dynamic conditions of a real attack, without hesitation, without panic and with intention, flesh-and-blood human predators, then his gun will be useless—

to him. It could, however, come in handy to the bad guy once the gun-owner is disarmed.

No weapon, whether artificial, like a gun or a knife, or natural, a specific striking technique or combination of techniques, should be fetishized.

As the great 17th century Japanese Samurai warrior, Musashi, said:

> *You should not have any special fondness for a particular weapon...Too much is the same as not enough.*

To ensure that one is as deadly as one needs to be with a gun, one should train in a martial system of some sort. Specifically, one should train one's body to become deadly.

Any who would object to this contention need look no further than the United States Marine Corps to see that it is sound. The USMC has instituted a martial arts program. It also has Marines train in bayonet fighting.

Why?

Well, it's certainly not because it is any longer expected that soldiers will be engaged in hand-to-hand combat on the battlefield, much less that they will be charging the enemy with bayonets. The virtue of these training modalities, though, develop in soldiers the mental fortitude, the moral will, needed to prevail over the enemy.

If you are training so as to deal with a man, up close and personally, who is determined to kill you, then you are training so that you won't think twice about stopping him by plunging a sharp instrument through his heart, or driving your thumbs through his eyeballs, or axe-hand chopping him in the throat with all of the tenacity and power that you would muster if you were trying to achieve the (admittedly anatomically impossible) task of decapitating him with your bare hand.

At this point, the gun becomes but an extension of your natural weaponry, your body, and the killing that much easier. An analogy: If you can drive a stick shift, then you can drive an automatic.

What's true for Marines is no less true for civilians, and civilians who are gun-owners.

It is never too late for law-abiding citizens to maximize to the full their odds of being able to successfully exercise their right, embodied in the Second Amendment to the United States Constitution, to defend themselves and their own from the wicked who would prey upon innocents.

ESSAY 4

Civilization and the Need to develop a Warrior Spirit

A FEW YEARS back, the law-abiding citizens of America had to contend with riots that were unprecedented in their country's history for the number of cities in which they occurred and the amount of damage that they caused. People, innocent people, were killed.

The riots have ended. But the rioters who unleashed the terror and their self-declared "allies" who exercised their influence to encourage and apologize for them at every turn have left in their wake a rise in violent crime in most major cities that shows little signs of abating any time soon.

The world is a dangerous place. This everyone has more or less always known. Recent events, though, have served as a reminder that civilization is more precarious than we're ordinarily inclined to think, for the violent will always be with us. This being so, whatever else the decent need to do in order to

31

preserve civilized life, they must, fundamentally, do one thing in the absence of which nothing else matters:

They must train to defend themselves.

Law abiding citizens must train physically and mentally in a real martial or combat art to make themselves into weapons of mass destruction that, at a moment's notice, can unleash upon any and all who would imperil them or their loved ones.

They must train their bodies and *wills* so that they can move with ruthless efficiency and *effortlessly* deliver bone-crushing strikes from any physiologically conceivable position.

They must train to cultivate within themselves the same raw, undifferentiated determination possessed by those in past times and places who fought, to the death, when necessary, to resist the predations of the ruthless.

American politics is a curious phenomenon. Partisans who continually purport to affirm the Individual over the State by referring back to the Declaration of Independence and the Second Amendment of the United States Constitution—and who invoke the Second Amendment as the means by which the "inalienable rights to life, liberty, and the pursuit of happiness" given by God are to be defended—don't ever call on people to assume responsibility for their own protection by not only exercising their "right to bear arms," but by habitually training their bodies and minds to become dangerous weapons themselves.

It's one thing to proclaim one's belief in some abstract principle embodied in the Second Amendment. It's another thing entirely to regularly encourage decent American citizens to train rigorously to become deadly to predators.

When it comes to nation-states, partisans of all stripes seem to have no problems realizing that only by projecting strength can one actor hope to deter attacks by others.

When it comes to individual actors, though, they apparently don't discern the applicability of this same principle.

There are at least two reasons for this:

First, for generations, the men and women of the West,

including even the most ardent exponents of "personal responsibility," have been conditioned to avoid doing or saying anything that could so much as remotely be construed as endorsing violence on the part of private citizens who only mean to exercise this personal responsibility in defense of the very rights that Western peoples pride themselves on promoting and safeguarding.

Yet there is another reason to account for why no advocates for "personal responsibility" and the Second Amendment can seem to muster the will to encourage individual Americans to, well, *assume individual responsibility* for their own protection.

The 17th century Japanese warrior Miyamoto Musashi issued the prescription to "perceive that which cannot be perceived with the eye." There is a distinction between perceiving what's possible with the mind's eye, as it were, and doing so with the literal eye. In other words, if you can't imagine it, if you don't believe or know that it could possibly exist or may even in fact exist, then even if it's right in front of you, you will not see it with your eyes.

And *this* is the situation within which those in the academic, media, and political classes find themselves. They don't encourage Americans to train in self-defense (of both the armed and unarmed varieties) precisely because *they themselves* haven't trained along these lines and, thus, can't conceive of the possibility of anyone who isn't an agent of the State competently defending themselves against aggressors.

It's simply not in their wheelhouse. They just aren't accustomed to thinking in terms of using violence in defense of themselves against aggressors, to say nothing of snapping the neck of an aggressor, or gouging the eyeballs out of his skull.

This, of course, isn't to suggest that they are *bad* or deceptive people because of this. It only means that a call for people to train to defend themselves is not an imaginable possibility for them.

Yet it can be. All that is necessary for this to occur is for them to resolve to remake themselves into, not *soldiers*, but *warriors.* Soldiers can be warriors, certainly, but a soldier is not necessarily a warrior just because he happens to be a soldier. And a warrior needn't be a soldier. This is distinction is crucial. It has been lost upon us. It must be restored.

To make themselves into warriors, people needn't join the military. What they must do is train in a true *martial* art, a combat art (not sport) that is designed to transform them in body and mind, a system designed to fundamentally transform them as people by not just instilling within them martial excellence, but the conviction that martial excellence *is* moral excellence.

To make themselves into warriors, all who advocate on behalf of personal responsibility, who claim to believe in rights to life and liberty and the Second Amendment that exists to secure these rights must train to acquire the physical skill and the moral resolve to neutralize, at whatever the cost, those who would violate these rights.

ESSAY 5

Managing Fear

FEAR.

Fear is the most primal and universal of all emotions, dwelling within all animal and human beings.

Yet it can be difficult, if not impossible, for many, particularly men, to talk about fear.

Fear is also politically profitable. Since the advent of the nation-state some five centuries ago, what the philosopher Michael Oakeshott referred to as "the politics of crisis" has been its lifeblood: politicians exploit it to elicit votes and campaign contributions from constituents, media corporations score high ratings and rake in billions of dollars in profits, and bureaucrats secure their careers while getting rich.

The fear whose flames are typically stroked by the usual suspects, though, is largely *irrational* fear.

Just as most of the fears that human beings have generally, or at least those over which they spend most of their time obsessing, are irrational.

Yet between fear that is rational and that which is not, there is all of the difference in the world—however difficult that is to grasp while snagged in the clutches of irrational fear.

Fear, when it is grounded in reality, when its object is something that *should* engender fright, is both necessary and desirable. Fear exists to keep us safe.

Most fear, though, particularly for the inhabitants of such technologically sophisticated and affluent societies as the United States, is not rational. Unique to human beings is that faculty known as *the Imagination*. A source of genius, creativity, and liberation from what were once regarded as the bounds of the possible, the Imagination, given its limitless ability to conjure up all manner of cataclysmic scenario can, when insufficiently disciplined, also be the well-spring of *terror*, of *irrational* fear.

Now—and this is critical—although the objects of fear produced by the Imagination are just thoughts, images, the fear to which they give rise is all too *real*. That the brain can't distinguish between that which is real and that which isn't is proven readily enough by consideration of the fact that both pleasant and unpleasant visualizations have the same *physiological* effects as their real, concrete counterparts.

This reason, then, why so many people spend years and even decades on the proverbial psychologist's couch with only minimal results is because the dominant self-help paradigm, with its almost exclusive focus upon the patient's mind, relies upon the dubious ontology of a mind-body dualism.

But the human being is not a duality of mind and body. The human being is a spiritual unity, a seamless oneness of body and mind. And when a person experiences fear, he experiences it *all throughout the body.*

So, when those who control the levers of influence succeed in cultivating fear within citizens, it assumes control over their entire being. Conservatives used to scoff at feminists when the latter insisted that "the personal is political." Yet if the analysis offered here is correct (as it is), then the feminists knew that of which they spoke—even if in spite of themselves.

So, what to do now?

First, recognize all of this. Recognize the primal character of fear, when it is rational and when it is not, its role as fuel in powering our politics, and, critically, its *physiological* nature.

Feel your fear the next time you begin to "stress" out.

Second, whether your fears are induced by political and media elites or from other aspects of everyday life, since you know that fear is experienced physically, to find your courage and surmount those fears it is imperative that you resolve them in your body.

It is imperative, in other words, to exercise.

But we'll go further. To conquer fear, it is ideal that one should *train* one's body in such a way as to accustom it to sustaining some measure of *trauma:* weightlifting, martial arts— these activities impact your body like few others. Unlike, say, football, they are activities of which people can continue to partake into old age.

The combat art of Warrior Flow is especially, indeed, *uniquely*, designed to assist students, of all ages, body-types, and levels of physical ability, to conquer their irrational fears by teaching them how to master their bodies' movement in such a way as to defend themselves against any and all prospective attackers with maximal efficiency.

Particularly given present circumstances, with crime rising and more Americans beginning to learn, or *re*learn, that the "personal responsibility" to which they routinely pay lip service and upon which they act in other areas of their lives entails *the obligation* to assume responsibility for their own defense, a look at a combat art, like the one I recommend, may not be a bad idea.

ESSAY 6

Lessons from Childhood for Politics: Fear and Bullying

FEAR.

The most primal and universal of emotions, it is preposterous to think that there are any of us who are immune to it.

It's at least as preposterous to think that *politics,* the activity of adjusting and continually readjusting human institutions so as to facilitate peaceful co-existence between a society's members, can somehow lay beyond fear's reach.

As Thomas Hobbes correctly recognized, politics are fundamentally grounded upon fear, the fear of violence, specifically the violent death that likely awaits human beings where there is no government.

Yet, particularly once people become adults, they do indeed think, or at least act and speak as if they think, that fear in no way accounts for their conduct. And nowhere is this self-delusion more prevalent than within the arena of contemporary political discourse.

Unquestionably, the rampant hypocrisy, flagrant contradictions, glaring inconsistencies, and blatant double standards that are the lifeblood of our political culture, though admittedly necessary for the advancement of material, ideological, and electoral interests, can also be accounted for in terms of the advancement of partisans' *psychological* interests.

This is key. When a person's incoherence proves intractable, and when intellectual and moral justifications collapse before they even take flight, it is to the psyches of those making them that our desire for intelligibility drives us.

Simply put, behind the moral exhibitionism, political partisans are at bottom motivated to do what they do because of their raw fears.

That this is true is gotten readily enough once we decide to view the world—i.e. people, including ourselves—as we viewed it when we were children and adolescents, before we permitted ourselves to be deluded by the seductive rhetoric and virtue-signaling of the actors in this venue we call "politics."

As children, we learn that some of our peers—bullies—succeed in the pursuit of their ends by way of subjecting other kids to violence (including threats of violence). We also learn of some other things: We learn either that most of those kids who are not directly victimized by the bully implicitly endorse the bullying by acquiescing, via silence, in the suffering of the bully's victims. Or they may assist the bully by allying with him, by going along-to-get along, for fear of becoming one of the bully's victims themselves.

Bullies, we learn early on, are typically treated with more sympathy than is meted out to their victims, and certainly much more so than is elicited from the quieter and "nerdier" kids.

Kids have no difficulty discerning the reason for this: It is fear.

Bullies provoke, and have every intention of provoking,

fear. They set out to dominate their environment through fear.

The political sphere has more than its share of bullies. Partisans, even as they purport to want peace and justice, seek to dominate by way of the perpetual threat of violence.

The violence needn't always be overt (although it increasingly is). The so-called "Cancel Culture" itself is an inherently coercive phenomenon, for by design it exists to visit upon its targets, not a literal, physical death, necessarily, but certainly a social one.

Persuasion or coercion: Outside of disengagement, these are our only two alternatives. Coercion, if it isn't a species of violence itself, is just a shade or two away from it. Almost always, partisan ideologues have shown that they prefer coercion to persuasion.

It's relatively rare for people to face that which they *truly* fear. Real fear is *felt* throughout a person's *body*. The object that provokes *that* experience is one that most (but definitely not all) people would prefer not to think about at all, much less reckon with in person.

So, rather than confront one's worst nightmare, and rather, then, to feel like a coward, a certain type of person would prefer to distract him *or herself* by conjuring up the proverbial windmill, a strawman, a bogeyman against which to rail.

Bullies in politics, like bullies in the schoolyard, would rather target those populations that are deemed more vulnerable than contend with more formidable forces. Nowhere are the double standards, the incivility, the "canceling," more evident today than within the realm of so-called "identity politics," i.e. politics that demand the endorsement of the race and gender ideologies that currently pervade our cultural institutions.

The self-professed guardians of these orthodoxies have chosen the path of least resistance, for they know that not only will they pay no price for selecting "the enemies" on whom they've chosen to set their sights. They, will, in fact, be generously rewarded for having made enemies of those with less political and social-cultural capital than themselves.

To put it simply, they have no more reason to fear those who they decry as obstacles to "progress" than a person who shadow boxes has to fear getting hit by his shadow.

Bullies, we learned as kids, will not bully those against whom bullying does not work. It won't work against other bullies.

Adults need to remember this.

ESSAY 7

This Thing Called "Fear"

FEAR.

Among the most universal and primal of all emotions, there is scarcely one among us who hasn't felt its presence. Perhaps this is why we seldom like to discuss it, at least when it comes to addressing our *own* fears.

Subjectively speaking, there is nothing pleasant about the experience of fear. Men especially are all too familiar with the discomfort of acknowledging, even to themselves, that there are things in the world that they fear, and this discomfort is never more acutely felt than when the objects of their fears are other men.

Notice, while it is neither possible nor desirable to rid ourselves of fear, it most certainly is possible to *manage* it—and to *use* it to make ourselves into better, stronger, happier people.

The first and most fundamental step toward managing fear is to *acknowledge* its presence within us.

The second step is to recognize that while there most certainly is an ineliminable, and quite profound, psychological component to fear, its physical component is no less significant, for fear is felt *within the body*. And it is often felt acutely, intensely. This being the case, to manage our fear, we must come to terms with its nature.

The experience of fear originates in the amygdala, an almond-shaped set of nuclei located in the temporal lobe of the brain that processes our emotions. When we encounter something that, say, frightens us, the amygdala activates. When it activates, it initiates activity in the hypothalamus, which in turn triggers the pituitary gland, the juncture at which the nervous and endocrine or hormone systems intersect.

It is at this point that the pituitary gland emits the adrenocorticotropic hormone (ACTH), the hormone that at once stimulates the adrenal cortex and provokes the body into releasing cortisol. The sympathetic nervous system—the system responsible for the "fight-or-flight response"—engages the adrenal gland and the latter injects epinephrine (or adrenaline) into the blood.

Cortisol, in addition to increasing blood pressure, blood sugar, and white blood cells, transforms fatty acids into the repository of energy for the muscles should a person decide to fight or flee.

The catecholamines of epinephrine, or adrenalin—a neurotransmitter which increases blood flow to the heart, lungs, and muscles—and norepinephrine or noradrenalin—the neurotransmitter that increases a person's heart rate and blood pressure—prime the body so as to make it as efficient and effective as possible in the event that violent action is necessary to combat the threat.

Yet making it as efficient and effective as possible to ward off a threat means that those processes that are necessary for immediate survival are ratcheted up, while those that aren't essential in the short-term are arrested. These "fear" hormones just mentioned dramatically diminish the workings of the gastrointestinal system, the digestive system, for the latter is not vital for the amount of time that it will take for a person to address a threat. This explains the queasiness, "the butterflies," that people experience in their stomachs when they are nervous, stressed, and fearful.

This as well leads to the "dry mouth" sensation that we experience while in a state of fear, for the salivary glands belong to the digestive system.

This is the physical phenomena constitutive of fear. Yet the modern study of fear confirms that its experience is no less *intellectual* or *psychological*. Two psychiatrists who co-authored an article that *The Smithsonian Magazine* reprinted note that:

> ...*some of the main chemicals that contribute to the 'fight or flight' response are also involved in other positive emotional states, such as happiness and excitement.*[1]

What they claim to have found throughout their own research, including their clinical interactions with patients, is that "what makes the difference between getting a 'rush' and feeling completely terrorized" is a rational assessment of "*context*." They write:

"When our 'thinking' brain gives feedback to our 'emotional' brain and we perceive ourselves as being in a safe space, we can then quickly shift the way we experience that high arousal state, going from one of fear to one of enjoyment or excitement."

To paraphrase the ancient Greek historian Herodotus, context is king. The hippocampus and prefrontal cortex engage in a complex, higher-order level of processing the context of a

---

[1] https://www.smithsonianmag.com/science-nature/what-happens-brain-feel-fear-180966992/

potential threat in order to determine whether it is an actual threat—see a paper called The Contextual Brain which illustrates the decisive role of context vis-à-vis fear.[2]

For example, if one were in the Arctic and somehow came within feet of a polar bear, one's response would be dramatically different than one's response to observing a polar bear in an exhibit at a zoo. Obviously, what accounts for these two radically different responses is an awareness of the radical difference between the one situation and the other.

Fear in and of itself isn't necessarily a choice, but how a person experiences fear and the manner in which he or she chooses to respond to it most certainly are choices. As such, these choices, as Aristotle correctly noted several centuries before Christ, possess both *rational* and *moral* value. A person who walks right up to a polar bear in the wild and thumps it in the nose is irrational in that he experiences, in Aristotle's terminology, a "*deficiency*" of fear. As such, he has the *vice*, the character weakness, of *recklessness*. Similarly, though, a person who is overcome by fear upon seeing a polar bear encased in a zoo exhibit is no less irrational. The only difference is that the latter has an "*excess*" of fear and suffers from the *vice*, or character weakness, of *cowardice*.

Both individuals are irrational inasmuch as they misinterpret or otherwise fail to attend to the contextual considerations that distinguish whether a threat is imaginary or whether it is real.

The presence of fear in itself in a person is nothing for which he or she should be ashamed. Fear is at once necessary and desirable, for fear alerts us to danger and mobilizes us to preserve our lives. In the absence of fear, the human species (along with every other whose members experience fear) would have long ago become extinct.

2

https://www.ncbi.nlm.nih.gov/pmc/articles/PMC5072129/?xid=P S_smithsonian

Neither, in itself, is fear something deserving of praise. Rather, the circumstances—the how, when, why, whom, and what—regarding a person's fear determine whether it is reasonable and, thus, commendable. It is the person who has habituated him or herself through education to *know* how to assess context and differentiate irrational fears from reasonable ones who distinguishes him or herself.

More in the future on this all-too neglected, but ubiquitous, phenomenon called "fear." For now, however, we should be encouraged, empowered, by knowing the fact that fear *is* manageable, and, once controlled, supplies an invaluable and even unique resource by which we can accomplish physical feats in the cause of self-protection and the protection of innocents that would otherwise remain the stuff of fantasy.

First and most fundamentally, though, we must come to terms with the blunt truth that we do indeed possess fear. Then, we should study it, as we began doing here. These are two essential steps toward managing fear.

Finally, we must train to own fear—rather than permit fear to own us.

ESSAY 8

The Need for "Ruthless Intent"

THE VIOLENCE THAT erupted on the streets of cities from coast-to-coast a few years back and the concerted effort on the part of sympathetic media and political figures to dismiss it all as a matter of "mostly peaceful protest," has underscored like few events in recent memory the need for law-abiding, peace-loving people to learn to defend themselves.

The endemic lawlessness and violence that engulfed hundreds of cities around the country had been followed by an 80% rise in the rate of gun sales. This being said, and while it is indeed a just and good thing that the Second Amendment is being exercised and that its exercise is being publicly encouraged by pundits and politicians of certain stripes, it's also noteworthy—and concerning—that little, if any, mention is ever made by these same public figures, or, for that matter, by most citizens themselves, of the need of a self-governing citizenry to cultivate a genuinely *martial* spirit, the mindset needed for ensuring the incapacitation of the bad guys before the bad guys have a chance to incapacitate the good guys.

A gun can be a great equalizer, for sure, but neither the possession of a gun nor even handiness with one is sufficient when confronted by determined, vicious attackers. Essential to self-defense is a mindset that the combat art of Warrior Flow refers to as "ruthless intent." [3]

Ruthless intent.

Founded by United States Marine Corps Lieutenant-Colonel Al Ridenhour, a combat veteran of both wars in Iraq and the war in Afghanistan and a marital artist of some 40 years, Warrior Flow is designed for one ultimate purpose.[4] It is meant to equip law-abiding citizens with both the physical ability and *the will* to "kill the bad guys," as Al has told all of his students from the moment they've had their first consultations with him.

"Martial" means "of or pertaining to war." Warrior Flow is a *martial* art in the literal and original sense of the term: Its students train for life-or-death situations, i.e. war.

In Warrior Flow, there are no uniforms, no aesthetically impressive, but essentially impractical, moves.

Training in Warrior Flow is most emphatically not training for contest or sport fighting.

Practitioners don't train, in other words, to confront *opponents* in *matches.*

They train to crush *enemies,* those who would prey upon them, their loved ones, and other innocents who may happen to be in their presence.

Training in Warrior Flow certainly involves training in weaponry (like firearms), but it is principally centered in the perfection of one's *natural weapons,* one's body.

While gun owners may scoff at the notion that any training in hand-to-hand combat is necessary when a gun can get the job

---

[3] https://protectyourself.mykajabi.com/

[4] https://moderncombatandsurvival.com/author/al-ridenhour/

done with far greater ease, this observation, though accurate as far as it goes, goes only so far, for the point is that, as Master Al is wont to continually remind his students, "Just because you have the most impressive and effective of tools, this doesn't make you a carpenter."

For example, the Marines still train with bayonets—even though they have long ceased to wage war on the battlefield with bayonets. So, why train with an antiquated weapon of war? The reason is simple: The more habituated one becomes to the idea of charging the enemy and driving a bayonet straight into his throat, the readier one will be to drop the enemy with a rifle from a distance.

Training in the use of bayonets cultivates the mindset of ruthless intent.

Ruthless intent is the mindset of the Warrior. Miyamato Musashi, an undefeated Japanese Samurai Warrior who lived nearly five centuries ago, provides us with as concise and clear a summation of ruthless intent as any when he instructs aspiring warriors to "*attack with the spirit of terror and death.*" [5]

Continuing, he writes:

> In the span of a single breath, crush your opponent's courage and cause him to tremble. Resolve in your heart to win under any circumstances and do not stop until the opponent is lying dead at your feet.

Musashi concludes:

> You must be direct and powerful and strike with speed and death.

So how does a decent, civilized, law-abiding citizen cultivate

---

[5] https://www.britannica.com/biography/Miyamoto-Musashi-Japanese-soldier-artist

ruthless intent? Like any other virtue—and, yes, despite the idea espoused by some combat instructors and theorists of war that combat is somehow "beyond good and evil," ruthless intent *is* a moral excellence, for it maximizes one's chances of victory over the purveyors of evil who would attack innocents—the cultivation of ruthless intent requires training.

Space constraints preclude a more thorough analysis here. A few brief remarks may suffice for now:

It is critical to develop constructive "self-talk." The idea of self-talk, of having the courage to delve within oneself, to dredge up one's implicit beliefs and prejudices, and to vigorously challenge them also happens to be one and the same idea as that at the heart of the philosophy of psychology that the famed Albert Ellis refers to as "Rational Emotive Behavioral Therapy."

All of us, to some degree or other, possess fear. Fear that is rational is both inescapable and good, for it alerts us to danger and keeps us alive.

Yet fear that is irrational is a plague.

The fear that most of us have—and that we've been *brainwashed* into having—is irrational. This fear in large measure stems from two things: (a) the moral ambiguity that's been instilled in us regarding good, evil, and the employment of violence; and the consequent (b) lack of confidence in one's own abilities to defend oneself against predators.

We've learned to have these thoughts, and our minds have, accordingly, conjured up scary images to go along with them.

But just as we have learned them, we can unlearn them, and adopt in their stead new thoughts and images.

Warrior Flow encourages students to reimagine themselves, to recognize in themselves their own self-worth as children of God who, as such, have an inalienable right to defend themselves by whichever means necessary against *anyone* who would prey upon innocents.

Bad people—those who unleash violence against innocents—are not "*opponents*"; they are *the Enemy*. In principle, real violence, the only sort of violence against which civilized human beings should prepare to defend themselves, is every bit as lethal as the violence that soldiers face on the battlefield. Thus, just as soldiers' training necessitates the objectification of their rivals as "the Enemy," so too, then, should those who train in self-defense do the same with respect to those who would threaten their lives. Now, those who prey upon innocents are not *your* enemy or *my* enemy, for to think in these terms is to risk taking things too personally. It encourages an impulse to *distance* oneself from an assailant, as one would be inclined to distance oneself from a rattlesnake or a Grisly bear. "*The* Enemy," on the other hand, being more abstract, less personal, removes the psychological mechanism that could impede one from closing the distance with an attacker. A defender can then regard the Enemy's body as his own to do with as he must in order to achieve victory over him.

Warrior Flow, via training in ruthless intent, fashions the law-abiding and the peace-loving into warriors whose aim is nothing more or less than the incapacitation of the uncivilized and violent by whichever means necessary.

Decent people need to defend themselves and one another. We increase our odds of doing this when we make it our aim to change ourselves into warriors, into men and women who have both the ability and the will to turn the predators into prey.

ESSAY 9

Thoughts on Guns, Violence, and Self-Protection

TRUE TO FORM, and without missing a beat, partisan opportunists used the murder of school children in Uvalde, Texas for their own political purposes.

This is but the latest episode in the seemingly perennial debate over guns.

Some food for thought:

First, notice that both gun-controllers and gun-enthusiasts make the same mistake: They both *anthropomorphize* an inanimate object. Both mystify the gun. Both fetishize it, treating it as if it was a "magic wand." For the gun-grabbers, it is the gun that is responsible for the damage that bad people inflict with it. For the gun-enthusiasts, the gun provides virtually absolute protection from bad people. "Well, if I'm attacked, I'll just grab my gun!" This is a common refrain among otherwise decent people who are just as guilty of personifying the gun as are the advocates of nonsensical gun legislation.

However, the gun, like any other tool, is a mindless, lifeless thing. It is only as effective as the person wielding it.

Second, the transformation of the gun into a talisman accounts for why gun enthusiasts equate, or at least seem to equate, the right to self-protection *exclusively* with the right to possess *guns*. It explains why being *disarmed* and being *without a gun* are regarded as mutually synonymous and, thus, why being without a gun is seen as the equivalent of being *defenseless*. Corporate media talking heads and scribblers perpetuate this fiction by headlining police shootings involving "unarmed" suspects—as if being unarmed means that a suspect isn't dangerous.

Third, that gun owners should wax hysterical over the prospect of being "disarmed" and, thus, rendered "defenseless" in the event that the government confiscates their guns should cause these gun owners to reconsider the wisdom of their decision to purchase a gun in the first place: Precisely because the gun is only as useful as the person to whom it belongs, a person who lacks the physical and, critically, *psychological* training to be as proficient as possible in the deployment of a firearm for the sake for which it exists—i.e. to kill assailants—is as much a danger to himself and other innocents as a child would be if it was in the hands of a child that a gun was placed.

At any rate, the mindset exhibited here, the mindset of hysteria and panic over the prospect that *anyone,* government employee or not, will disarm and render defenseless legal gun owners, is most definitely not that of the warrior.

While there is no shortage of appeals to the Constitution in the cause of advancing gun rights, the *example* of *the men who bequeathed* the Constitution is seldom consulted. What did the Founders *do* when *they* believed that their liberties were being violated?

The question, being rhetorical, speaks for itself, for we know from history that when the members of the Generation of

1776 felt that *their* government had crossed a line from which there was no turning back, they went all in, putting their lives, fortunes, and sacred honors on the line in order to defend their rights, the rights of free agents endowed by their Creator with "unalienable rights." When their initial attempt to peaceably secede was met with resistance, it was only then that they went to war.

Fourth, while secession is indeed as American as apple pie, and it is an intrinsically peaceful means of conflict-management baked into the cake of the Constitution of *these* United States, and while war, too, is, in principle, permissible as long as it is the last option after all others have been exhausted, neither course of action is possible or desirable at this moment in time. Moreover, both secession and war are *collective* enterprises that, as such, make the well-being of the *individual* contingent upon the success of others—*lots* of others. However, it is this disposition to turn toward sources outside of oneself for one's happiness, a disposition whose development is encouraged at every turn by our political culture that is the problem.

At the end of the day, adult men and women must reckon with the fact that it is they alone who are responsible for their own well-being. Miyamoto Musashi, a 17th century Japanese Samurai warrior, put the point well:

> *There is nothing outside of yourself that can ever enable you to get better, stronger, richer, quicker, or smarter. Everything is within. Everything exists. Seek nothing outside of yourself.*

Political junkies, even when they are talking the talk of "personal responsibility" and "individualism," fail to recognize just how disempowering political engagement can be. They fail to appreciate the extent to which they've been conditioned to discern problems—potentially cataclysmic crises—everywhere that they look, emergencies whose solutions always lie in the future and that can be achieved only by others. In execution, if not necessarily in conception, American politics cultivates in those who fall under its spell a proclivity to focus upon what they *lack*, and the belief in a type of *messianism*, the belief that they can be made whole only by way of politicians—euphemistically regarded as "leaders"—who they must elect and re-elect.

It is this worldview, we submit, that accounts for the default response of so many gun owners to the threat, perceived or imagined, that they may be disarmed. They turn to something outside of themselves, the gun, for their protection. If, though, they absorbed the gun into themselves, so to speak; if they trained physically and psychologically to *become* the gun, to become the death of the bipedal vermin that prey upon innocents, then they would recognize that the gun—like any other artificial weapon of which they may avail themselves—is but an extension of their natural weaponry, their minds and bodies. The gun, then, will basically be along for the ride.

Ditto for a knife, sword, club, stick, pipe, or any other inanimate object used by a defender to defeat an attack.

Though Musashi would eventually open his own school of sword fighting, it should be obvious to those who are acquainted with his written work that this undefeated Samurai warrior was not, fundamentally, preoccupied with *swords*. Rather, he recognized that martial mastery requires the perfection of a set of physical and psychological traits—martial virtues—in the absence of which no one could be trained to wield a sword (or any other instrument) effectively. *Maximal economy of bodily motion* and *a will* focused upon striking the enemy with *merciless intention* are the necessary and sufficient ingredients in the recipe for victory. Neither artificial weapons *nor the* "*techniques*" with which contemporary martial artists are overwhelmingly preoccupied are fundamental: For example, in order for one to be able to execute, say, a hammer punch under the dynamic conditions of a real-world attack, one must have trained one's body to move as efficiently, as subtly, as *deceptively,* as possible, and, in order to do *that,* one must spend comparable time shaping within one's psyche the intention to critically injure, maim, and *destroy* the enemy. The two are inseparable, for how we think influences how we feel, and how we think and feel influences how we move, which in turn influences how we think, and how we feel, and so on and on.

The takeaway here is that rather than partake of the perpetual collective bitch fest that *is* contemporary partisan politics, there are steps that individuals can take *right now* to enrich their own lives. And they don't need politicians and pundits who promise them a better state of affairs in some distant future to do it.

The politics of victimhood is correctly condemned. Unfortunately, its critics, at least when it comes to the issue of gun rights, often prove themselves to be purveyors of this kind of politics themselves. This will remain the case until and unless they stop speaking and acting as if their right, their *obligation,* to defend themselves, and defend themselves and their loved ones via firearms, is even remotely negotiable.

And they will abandon this disposition when they reconcile themselves with the brute fact that it will be by whatever means necessary that they will protect themselves and other innocents within their care from the predations of the violent. Until then, they will continue to be anxious over the prospect that their government will "disarm" them.

When, however, a person has trained himself to feel in the very marrow of his being that no one, whether one or many and regardless of position and power, is going to have any more luck depriving him of his right to defend himself and his family than they'd succeed in coercing him or his children to board a train destined for a concentration camp—well, this is a total game-changer. It's a different mindset.

It's a warrior mindset.

ESSAY 11

Rising Crime, Self-Protection, and Finding Honest Martial Instruction

SINCE THE EXPLOSION of lawlessness and violence that marked that horrible summer of 2020, crime has risen precipitously in cities throughout the country. This alone should be sufficient to convince decent American citizens to train in self-protection. Yet those who are interested in doing so should be cautious lest they fall victim to, as Richard Feynman referred to it, "the ignorance of experts."

Regrettably, it doesn't take much of a critical eye to discern that of the seemingly endless supply of martial arts instructors whose demonstrations can be found on YouTube, far too many of them convey, at best, mixed messaging. At worst, they are demoralizing.

In any event, they set their students up for failure.

A particularly instructive illustration of this phenomenon is an exchange that occurred between two skilled martial artists, former Navy Seal, Jocko Willink, and Tim Kennedy, an Army Ranger.[6] Kennedy was a guest on Willink's podcast and the question of how a "non-fighter" should train for self-defense was posed to the two special operators by a viewer.

The host turned the query over to his guest. "Anything is better than nothing," Kennedy insisted. Even "*Crossfit training*," given its self-defense component, is a viable option. However, while there's not "a right or a wrong" course of action to take when it comes to training in self-defense, there *are* "degrees of better."

For Kennedy, one can't go wrong with the "foundational martial arts," i.e. "wrestling, boxing, Muay Thai, and Jiu Jitsu." Elaborating, he stated: "You know, you step up against a guy that has a little bit of knowledge in any one of those…they're a pain in the ass. And if he has a little bit [of knowledge] in all of them or he's really good at one of them? Just kiss your ass goodbye. You're going to sleep."

Willink unequivocally agreed. Yet he also informed his sizable audience that they already have a "natural defense"— which is to "run away." If someone comes at me and "you've got a knife, or whatever," Willink said, "I'm going to run from you. It's okay. It's defense. I'm being defensive. I'm running away from you."

Kennedy replied: "I 100% agree with you." He added that if someone came up to him and demanded that he give him his wallet, Kennedy would reply: "You've got to catch me first."

Tim Kennedy and Jocko Willink are representative of an attitude that pervades the contemporary world of the martial arts. To be sure, while martial artists generally, and Tim Kennedy and Jocko Willink specifically, are indeed the good guys, the attitude distilled here fails to do justice to the concerns of those who turn to them as authorities on the subject of self-protection and who rely upon them for assistance in helping them surmount their own fears of being preyed upon.

To respectfully and honestly address the inquiries of prospective martial arts students, a martial arts instructor must ask and answer for himself the following questions:

1. *What* is a martial art?
2. What is *the context* within which I will prepare my students to use violence?
3. *Against whom* am I preparing students to use the skills that I instill in them?
4. *To whom,* exactly, will I impart this training?
5. *What,* psychologically speaking, motivates people to pursue training in a martial art?
6. How will I do right by my students in satisfying this psychological longing?

What is a Martial Art?

Let's get back to basics and remind ourselves that "martial," as in *martial* art, means "of or pertaining to *war.*"

War.

The martial arts, then, are, historically and etymologically, the arts of war.

Martial arts instructors, then, have a singular task vis-à-vis their students: They must instill martial prowess, i.e. the skill and the will to incapacitate the enemy by whatever means necessary. The violence for which a student of a real martial art trains is the violence that is necessary to wield in order to prevail in a conflict that could become lethal.

What is the Context within which Martial Arts Students will Prepare Themselves to Use Violence?

Given the definition of a martial art, the only appropriate training modality is one that prepares students to unleash violence within the context of a potentially life-threatening attack launched by a determined assailant against innocents, whether those innocents are students themselves, their loved ones, or other innocents who can't fend for themselves.

To put it another way, martial arts students should not be training for duels, matches, contests, or bar or street brawls. They should not, in other words, train to *brawl* at all, and for the same reason that soldiers don't train for such adolescent bullshit. And, like soldiers, students of the martial arts, then, should train to dispatch of potentially homicidal assailants with ruthless efficiency.

Students pursuing self-protection training in a martial art should be trained to encounter, not "*opponents*" but, rather, "*enemies.*"

There are only *enemies*, anti-humans who have divested themselves of their humanity by choosing instead to become bipedal predators who feed off of the blood of innocents.

Against Whom am I Preparing Students to use the Skills that I Instill in Them?

To repeat the last point: Students should be training to become as capable as possible of *destroying* the enemy. And the enemy is anyone who won't think twice about raping, robbing, bludgeoning, and murdering innocents in order to get what he wants.

Let's put this another way: Students are not training to win contests. They're not training for sport. The enemy is not likely to be an athlete, a boxer, or another martial artist. Nor should students be training to kick the ass of some guy who is acting like a douchebag.

In other words, boxing, wrestling, Muay Thai, BJJ—the arts that Tim Kennedy and Jocko Willink recommend for those who are interested in learning self-protection—presuppose a context fundamentally other than the context of a martial art, the context of *war*. They presuppose an opponent, someone with whom one can "square off" or with whom it is safe to go to the ground. This assumption is at once wholly intelligible and appropriate within the context of a sport. It couldn't be more inappropriate, more dangerous, within the context of a possibly deadly confrontation, of war.

As far as grappling is concerned, most of the pioneers of World War II Close Quarter Combatives were grapplers. So too were many of their students. And yet they have always insisted, forcefully and repeatedly, that the ground is the *last* place to which one wants to go in a real violent confrontation—however masterful a "ground game" one may have achieved. The ground, given its solidity and the potential it has to be uneven and strewn with debris and broken glass, isn't remotely as accommodating as a mat in a dojo. And considering the likelihood that the enemy could have a weapon and/or fellow belligerents waiting in the wings to whom a defender will be that much more vulnerable while on the ground, training in a grappling art leaves much to be desired for the only kind of (non-sportive) confrontation for which decent civilian adults should ever prepare.

When we turn to the standing arts, things are not much better.

The conventional fighting stance that students of boxing and many other martial arts are taught to assume reinforces this fiction—an invidious fiction—that it is some single opponent against whom they'll be "squaring off."

Yet squaring off, putting up one's dukes, is likely to be neither necessary nor desirable against a scumbag or gang of scumbags who are resolved to cave in the side of your skull with a crowbar or a tire iron, or who sucker strikes you in the back of your head with a rock.

The point is that the only type of violent transaction for which it is both morally and *legally* permissible for adults to engage occurs everywhere but comes from nowhere. It is a life or death situation, whether or not the assailant or assailants intend to extinguish the lives of their targets. There's nothing sporty or organized about it.

Since, then, microseconds count, it should be obvious that there is no time for a person targeted to square off. Not only is it not likely that there would be time to do so while under attack. Even if there was time to do so, it would be a *waste* of time, for it takes more time to stand in a guard position and then strike than it takes to just strike!

And by throwing up the hands in front of one's head and face prior to pre-empting the enemy's assault, one renders exponentially more difficult to sustain any argument from self-defense one may try making upon severely injuring or killing an assailant. This is because if one had time to assume a conventional fighting stance, then, presumably, one had time to walk away or otherwise diffuse the confrontation. In squaring off, one consents to "fight."

Again, in a ring or within the context of sport, this make sense. In the context of self-protection, it most assuredly does not.

So, to put it simply and contrary to Tim Kennedy's suggestion, a person is not likely to be violently attacked by a practitioner of boxing, wrestling, Muay Thai, or Jiu Jitsu. One must train accordingly.

To Whom will I Impart this Training?

The people most likely to pursue training in an art of war for the sake of defending themselves and their loved ones generally possess various peculiar characteristics.

First of all, while they can be of any age, those who are seeking training in a combat art tend to be, not necessarily old, but old*er*.

Since they want to learn how to maximize their odds of being able to successfully defend themselves within their unique bodies, they are not aiming to compete, so styles and systems that specialize in flashy, choreographed, but largely impractical techniques are not going to appeal to them.

Second, they are not, then, likely to be especially athletic, if they're athletic at all. Again, it is not for the purpose of becoming more athletic, of increasing, say, their endurance, burning calories, etc. that students of a martial art train.

Every drill, every habit sown, must be conducive to the end of making students ever more efficient at neutralizing those who would prey upon them.

Third, they are most definitely *not* troublemakers. This being the case, they don't need for their instructor to repeatedly warn them against using the skills they acquire in their training for nefarious or otherwise illegitimate purposes.

Nor do they need to have the very fears that motivated them to pursue martial training in the first place reinforced by the people—their instructors—to whom they turn for help in *surmounting* their fears!

What this means is that instructors who go about with a long face, as if they lament having to train their students in the use of violence, who indiscriminately (without any attention paid to circumstances) tell their students to *run,* and who deluge them with ominous tales of the "prison-trained monsters" up against whom they may come further ensconce the anxieties, and possibly the trauma, that motivated their students to take up the study of self-protection.

They do their students a grave injustice by failing to deliver the goods.

What, Psychologically Speaking, Motivates People to Pursue training in a Martial Art?

To reiterate the last point, it is *fear,* the fear of not being able to successfully defend oneself and one's loved ones from verminous bipedal predators that fundamentally accounts for why your average person, particularly your average adult, takes up the study of a martial art.

This being the case, instructors have an obligation to help their students manage and channel that fear for the purpose of annihilating the enemy, if the occasion should ever demand this course of action.

Instructors who fail to know their students by strengthening this fear *fail their students.*

How will I do Right by my Students in Satisfying this Longing?

Instructors fulfill their calling by, well, at the very least, refusing to peddle fear porn consisting of tales of invincible bad guys, life imprisonment for decent people who defend themselves and their loved ones from the bad guys, and orders to run from the bad guys!

Yet they have a duty to do more.

Martial arts instructors need to spare no occasion to instill in their students both the physical skill and, critically, the moral will, the mental focus, to excise from the planet like the malignant cancer that they are any and all who would imperil the innocent.

Period.

The enemy is *not* invincible. He's mortal. Whatever his race, religion, or tribe, and whether he is a drug kingpin, a terrorist, a mafia hitman, a gangbanger, or an ex-con—the enemy bleeds, breaks, and dies.

He can be critically injured, maimed, and killed.

Instructors should continually remind their students of this axiomatic truth. Students of the martial arts, specifically, the arts of war, don't need to be told about how dangerous such low lives are (as if they would go around looking to pick "fights" with these types, or *any types,* once they got a little training in a warrior art under their belt!). They need to have it drilled into them that the Godless are not only mortal but will in fact be forced to come to terms with their mortality if the evil are ever so stupid as to attack them!

This is the martial spirit. We need more of it in the world of the martial arts.

And those American citizens who are willing to assume responsibility for their own protection by pursuing the study of a genuinely martial art should take care to seek out an instructor who has asked and answered the foregoing questions.

ESSAY 12

More on Ruthless Intent

RUTHLESS INTENT IS the term that the combat art of Warrior Flow uses to characterize the mentality that it aims to instill in its students.[7]

Ruthless Intent, to put it simply, is the will to kill would-be murderers, rapists, and other violent thugs who target innocents. The training of Warrior Flow practitioners, like that of warriors from around the world and throughout history, necessarily includes mental as well as physical development.

It necessarily includes the cultivation of Ruthless Intent.

Contrary to what many, including, sadly, most martial artists (and combat artists to boot!) are inclined to think, Ruthless Intent is neither immoral nor amoral. It is a *virtue,* a *martial* virtue, a moral excellence that, intrinsic as it is to the proper exercise of the right of self-defense, is inseparable from the affirmation of

---

[7] https://protectyourself.mykajabi.com/

human life itself.

Ancient and medieval ethicists knew that moral education consisted in learning by example, by emulating, even if not consciously, those who embodied strengths of character. With an eye toward the end of developing the virtue of Ruthless Intent, we would be well-served to turn our attention to Miyamoto Musashi (1584-1645).

A Warrior-Scholar, Musashi was an undefeated swordsman with 61 duels under his belt. Many of these, particularly in his younger days, ended in the demise of Musashi's enemies. At 13, when he engaged in his first confrontation, the young boy charged Arima Kihei, an adult who Musashi would later describe as "a sword adept" of a specific school. William Scott Wilson, author of *The Lone Samurai,* explains what happened:

When Musashi's uncle, Dorin, was pleading with Kihei to call off the duel due to his nephew's age, Musashi "charged Kihei with a six-foot quarterstaff[8] [a wooden staff] shouting a challenge to Kihei." The latter, in turn, "attacked with a wakizashi[9] [a sword]...." Musashi slammed him on the ground, and when Kihei tried to regain his footing, Musashi blasted him between the eyes and then beat him to death.

An account of another duel in which Musashi engaged later in life, when he was 28, shows that Ruthless Intent is not the same thing as blind rage. In fact, it *precludes* rage. It requires a calmness of mind and spirit.

Sasaki Kojiro was among Japan's greatest Samurais. His speed and precision were unsurpassed. His weapon of choice was "a huge no-dachi blade, a curved Japanese sword in the classic style, but with a blade over a meter in length." Given its "size and weight," it was "a brutal, unsubtle weapon [.]" Nevertheless, Kojiro "had perfected its use to a degree unheard of in all Japan."

Musashi challenged him to a duel. Kojiro accepted. On the

---

[8] https://en.wikipedia.org/wiki/B%C5%8D
[9] https://en.wikipedia.org/wiki/Wakizashi

morning of April 13, 1612, they were scheduled to meet on a beach. Kojiro was there earlier with his retinue. He would periodically interrupt his time in meditation by sipping tea, making small talk, and laughing with his entourage as they all awaited the arrival of the man who they were confident Kojiro would effortlessly decimate.

Yet Kojiro's demeanor underwent a dramatic change as hour rolled into hour and Musashi failed to show. Kojiro became agitated. Then he became enraged. Musashi was now over three hours late. This tardiness Kojiro viewed as an offense against his honor.

What neither he nor any of his students and servants who were with him realized, though, is that Musashi had been nearby the entire time. Musashi hired an elderly man with a boat to sail him to just beyond sight of Kojiro. For hours, he calmly carved one of the man's spare oars into a bokken, a wooden staff. Once Musashi had completed his task, he had the man row him over to confront Kojiro.

When Kojiro caught sight of the boat, it took him a few seconds or so to realize that Musashi was in it. As it drew nearer and Musashi leapt into the water. Kojiro ran toward him. He was disoriented for a moment as he noticed that Musashi didn't even have a sword. At that moment, he swung his no-dachi, but Musashi moved just enough—literally centimeters—and avoided being struck. Kojiro overcommitted, for by the time that he regrouped to bring his blade down upon the skull of Musashi, the latter...*disappeared.*

Of course, Musashi did not literally disappear. Rather, upon having gotten under Kojiro's guard, he had dashed to the right and blasted Kojiro with his bokken.

The fight had been over before it started, for Musashi been ahead of Kojiro's movement from the beginning. But it was at this particular juncture that Kojiro's defeat started to unfold.

Once Musashi hit him, Kojiro started to flail, swinging his sword wildly. Musashi then smashed him in the skull before shattering his ribs. Kojiro couldn't breathe as he felt the inside of his chest exploding.

Kojiro's following watched in disbelief as their Master dropped dead on the sands of the beach.

Musashi seemed about ready to engage them. Instead, he ran back toward the boat in which he arrived and sailed off. Reportedly, he cried over having ended the life of such a distinguished Samurai warrior. Musashi would continue to teach the art of swordsmanship for the remainder of his life. He would never lose a duel, but he would never again take the lives of any of his opponents.

What this story illustrates is that Musashi showed Ruthless Intent—but no rage. He didn't even seem to have any anger at all.

Musashi's willingness to spare the lives of those of his opponents who he would defeat in the future underscores another feature of Ruthless Intent: It expands its possessor's range of options.

While Ruthless Intent is indeed the will to crush the enemy, the person who exercises his will to defeat the enemy need not necessarily destroy him. He can choose, in accordance with his own practical wisdom, his own knowledge of the specific circumstances in which he finds himself, to allow the Enemy to live.

Before closing, it is worthwhile to consider some quotations from this great exemplar of the martial virtue of Ruthless Intent:

> *The primary thing when you take a sword in your hands is your intention to cut the enemy, whatever the means.*
>
> *When you decide to attack, keep calm and dash in quickly, forestalling the enemy...attack with a feeling of constantly crushing the enemy, from first to last.*
>
> *To become the enemy, see yourself as the enemy of the enemy.*
>
> *Approach the enemy with the attitude of defeating*

him without delay.

When the enemy starts to collapse you must pursue him without the chance of letting go. If you fail to take advantage of your enemies' collapse, they may recover.

When you attack the enemy, your spirit must go to the extent of pulling the stakes out of a wall and using them as spears and halberds.

Let go of your thoughts and let your spirit direct you. Set your mind at ease and do not think about how to attack, just attack with the spirit of terror and death. In the span of a single breath, crush your opponent's courage and cause him to tremble. Resolve in your heart to win under any circumstances and do not stop until the opponent is lying dead at your feet.

From Miyamoto Musashi, we can learn much about the life-affirming martial virtue of Ruthless Intent.

ESSAY 13

Ruthless Intent: It's Cultivation

WARRIORS AREN'T BORN. They are made.

This is the philosophy behind Warrior Flow Combatives, or Warrior Flow.

And a Warrior without *Ruthless Intent* is like a library without books or, more accurate yet, a square without four sides.

Ruthless Intent is nothing more or less than *the will* to crush *the Enemy*, those who would prey upon the innocent.

To the end of cultivating this virtue—and, yes, it most certainly is a martial *and moral* virtue—physical training is necessary, yes. But even more importantly, mental training is required.

To cultivate Ruthless Intent, the aspiring Warrior must routinely engage in three mutually supportive and equally essential activities: *Self-Talk, Visualization,* and what Warrior Flow refers to as *Visceralization."*

Self-talk requires one to pay meticulous attention to the

71

inner commentary that the mind ceaselessly cranks out, for even when it is commentary upon happenings in the external world, it is, ultimately, *autobiographical*, it is *self*-commentary, for our thoughts on the world, our relationships with others, are inescapably colored and shaped by our experiences and memories.

We need to manage that "inner voice."

Self-talk is inescapable. We are all incessantly speaking to ourselves, whether we realize it or not. There is scarcely a moment when, either through word or image, we aren't communicating to ourselves. Past experiences, or our interpretations of those experiences, we have, in large measure subconsciously, weaved into an autobiographical narrative. As is the case with any other work, our self-story is necessarily selectively edited. Yet we confuse this highly redacted version of ourselves with our whole selves.

And we allow this abridged reading of ourselves to color our sense of reality.

Warrior Flow implores students to attend carefully to their Self-Talk. Moreover, they are to assume conscious control of it, to habituate their minds to thinking self-affirming thoughts. In the case of this combat art specifically, the Warrior-in-the-Making must begin thinking and living as if the future self that he wants to become is already a present reality.

It doesn't demand much reflection to realize that this is indeed how we became whatever it is that we've ever become. If one wants to become a cook, one must first cook. If one wants to become a dancer, one must dance. If one wants to become a football player, one must play football.

Aristotle, the most prominent of all virtue theorists, wrote famously on this subject. Brave men become brave by *acting like brave men*. Just men become just by *acting like just men*.

Comprehensively, virtuous people become virtuous by *acting virtuously*.

Similarly, one becomes a warrior by acting like one. And

acting like a warrior means as well thinking like one.

Yet Aristotle knew that being virtuous was a matter not just of *thinking* a certain way, but of *feeling* the appropriate way. For instance, a courageous person is someone who knows what to fear and *the extent to which he should fear it*. The object of fear elicits the emotion or passion of fear within the body. The courageous person, though, experiences fear in the appropriate proportion.

The aspiring warrior must *feel* as the Warrior that he will become feels. As he regularly affirms his own physical abilities, his resolute acceptance of injury, and even death, in battle, and his equal resolve to incapacitate the Enemy by whichever means, with ruthless efficiency, his Self-Talk will necessarily be accompanied by visuals.

As with his Self-Talk, though, the Warrior Within must make sure that the activity of Visualization in which he engages is consciously directed. He needs to open up the reservoir of his imagination and unleash his creative powers as he envisions himself crucifying, without mercy, the monsters of his choosing. They could be real people or imaginary. They can be people who one has personally known or only those of whom one has heard. In any event, to cultivate Ruthless Intent—the conviction that predators *must* be reduced to prey, the raw, undifferentiated determination to instill within violent attackers the same unbridled terror that they sought to inspire in their victims—one must not only *visualize,* but *visceralize.*

Visceralization includes visualization, but extends beyond it to encompass the other senses. When a person engages in visceralization, he doesn't just *see* the object of his imagination; he hears, smells, and touches it, perceiving it with painstaking detail. Or we could say that to visceralize is to engage in what students of Neuro Linguistic Programming (NLP) refer to as "*associated* visualization."

In other words, when associated visualization or visceralization occurs, the visualizer doesn't just form a mental picture of himself within the framework of the visual, as is the case when it is "*dissociated* visualization" that occurs. Associated visualization, in contrast, *immerses* the visualizer within the scene that he envisages, allowing him to enact it.

When a person visceralizes, he experiences those emotions that he either once experienced, if he is reliving a past event, or those that he would experience if the event that he visceralizes actually occurred. Physiologically speaking, the emotion felt in the body while visceralizing and that felt in response to a real world happening are one and the same. The brain doesn't know the difference.

Specifically, when developing Ruthless Intent, an aspiring warrior must not only perceive in his mind his attacker or attackers; he must as well *feel* in the very marrow of his bones all of the contempt, the righteous indignation and fury with which he envisions himself destroying the Enemy. Physiologically speaking, the feelings that he conjures while training are one and the same as those that he would have in a real confrontation. The brain doesn't know the difference between the fantasy and the reality.

While engaged in visceralization, the aspiring Warrior can, for example, feel the flesh of the Enemy's neck spontaneously with the sound of it snapping as he drives an axe-handed chop to it with all of the power that he believes is necessary for the purpose of cleaving the Enemy's skull from the rest of his body. Beholding the (admittedly anatomically impossible) spectacle of decapitating the Enemy's head with the side of his hand promises to go no small distance toward marshalling and channeling from within one's pain, rage, fear, and disdain for the wicked.

There's a practically limitless number of ways by which the Warrior-in-Waiting can visceralize visiting destruction upon the Enemy. He can, in reality, press his own thumbs against his own eyes and then take that vivid impression and imagine gouging out with those same thumbs the eyeballs of the Enemy. Imagining the soft lumpiness of the Enemy's eyeballs, the aspiring Warrior can visceralize ripping them out of his skull as he tears with his teeth, with all of the tenacity of a pit bull, substantial chunks of the Enemy's neck where the jugular vein is located.

Creativity in combat is a virtue of the Warrior. Yet it presupposes Ruthless Intent.

And to the end of cultivating Ruthless Intent, Self-Talk, Visualization, and Visceralization are imperative.

ESSAY 14

On Manhood: The Warrior Part I

IN A PREVIOUS essay, we argued that our contemporary culture offers males in search of manhood few viable models.[10]

Fortunately, all is not lost. But in order to realize his potential as a man *in the future*, a male must first turn his attention *to the past,* to an ideal type of Manhood with a pedigree that transcends time and place.

It is history, that of both Western and other peoples, that presents males today with the ideal of **the Warrior.**

Tellingly, there is something on the order of a cross-cultural, trans-historical consensus on the nature of the Warrior. The minds of men separated by centuries and geography, inhabiting different universes, are as one when it comes to the subject of the characteristics that distinguish the Warrior from all others.

---

[10] https://townhall.com/columnists/jackkerwick/2020/02/04/on-manhood-some-dominant-wrong-models-n2560667

Crucially, physical prowess, though *necessary*, is far from *sufficient* to make one a Warrior. The Warrior must also possess intellectual excellence.

Thus, the term "Warrior-*Scholar*" is meaningless because it is redundant: It has always been understood that a Warrior, by definition, must be educated.

Thucydides, recognized as among the first historians, has been credited (whether properly or not is beside the point) with having summarized this idea thus:

"The Nation that makes a great distinction between its scholars and its warriors will have its thinking done by cowards and its fighting done by fools."

To be clear, a "scholar," within this context, is not necessarily someone who teaches at a university or publishes in academic journals. These activities we associate with scholarliness, it is true. But the scholarliness of the Warrior, it has traditionally been understood, finds expression in his intellectual virtues, those of his mental habits that have been sewn through both his physical training as well as his education into the various arts.

It's critical to realize, though, that the Warrior insists upon the cultivation of his mind, *not* for the sake of some abstract ideal of learning for its own sake; the Warrior does not recognize any distinction between theory and practice, mind and body. Quite the contrary: There are two, ultimately inseparable, reasons for why it has always been held that a Warrior without erudition is like a library without books, or a square without four sides:

Firstly, Warriors around the globe knew long before the Jewish philosopher Hannah Arendt would argue for this thesis in the 20th century that between *thinking* and *morality* there is an indissoluble connection.

Arendt and her family fled from their native Germany after Hitler and his Nazis had risen to power. After the war, Arendt attended the trial of Adolph Eichmann, the architect of the Holocaust. What she claimed to have observed is that Eichmann, who justified his conduct on the grounds that he was simply "following orders," wasn't at all the monster that she expected to see. Rather, he exhibited what Arendt memorably described as "a curious, but quite authentic, *inability to think*."

The inability to think, it is clear from Arendt's work, isn't necessarily a literal *inability*. And it certainly isn't peculiar to Eichmann and Nazis. It is actually the *unwillingness* to think critically, the unwillingness to think beyond the bumper-sticker slogans—the stock phrases, clichés, and conventionalities—of the times.

Eichmann's inability or unwillingness to think resulted in his committing evil at the behest of a superior in the chain of command. The inability or unwillingness to think on the part of a democrat (small "d," notice), amounting as it does to an eagerness to be a herd animal, a mental conformist, or a sheep, can result in his committing evil as he goes along to get along with the mob. Right action depends upon clear thinking, an educated mind forms a virtuous character—this the Warrior has always known well. The Vikings had a saying that succinctly encapsulates this insight:

"Even in the sheath the sword must be sharp—so too must the mind and the spirit be within the body."

As Arendt noted, no less a figure than Socrates himself not only discerned, but aspired to embody in his person, the connection between thinking and morality. This is significant, for while it is easy to forget, the fact is that Socrates was a *warrior*.

The same man who famously stated that "the unexamined life is not worth living" was not only a *decorated* war hero, but a *celebrated* one. During the Peloponnesian War (which raged for about 27 years), Socrates, who may have been as old as 48 years of age by this time, served gallantly. Multiple battles served as occasions for him to showcase his martial prowess.

Yet for Socrates, who insisted that it is always better to suffer wrongdoing than to commit it, the exhibition of martial prowess in the service of a just cause, like the just cause of the protection of his beloved Athens that he was convinced he advanced, is the function of moral excellence.

The idea that war is somehow outside the boundaries of morality—an idea that is far too prevalent nowadays—is one that neither Socrates nor any other warrior could fathom.

Secondly, the Warrior values the development of his mind as much as his body because of his particular vision of the person as a *unity* of body *and* mind.

In other words, the Warrior sees the human being as a *spiritual unity*.

All that this last point means is that the Warrior ethos resolutely excludes that view of the human being entailed by contemporary Western atheism.

It is radically incompatible, in other words, with what's known as *materialism*, the metaphysical doctrine which asserts that there is no spirit, soul, or mind, that all things are simply matter in motion.

The Warrior ethos is incompatible with materialism not just because the Warrior denies its truth—we are, after all, more than worm food—but as well because materialism all too readily gives rise to hedonism and egoism, the doctrines, respectively, that pleasure and the self are the greatest of all goods.

The Warrior, in glaring contrast, is committed to a life of self-transcendence. He recognizes a spiritual order that has purchased a claim upon him. For the Warrior who is Jewish, Christian, or Islamic, it is, ultimately, for the sake of God that he enthusiastically sheds blood, both that of the enemy and, if need be, that of his own.

Yet one who lacks a belief in God, or Heaven, does not necessarily lack a belief in a transcendent spiritual realm (although we would argue, and have argued, that the logic of the concept of the spiritual points inexorably to God).

The Warrior who defends his people, his tribe, his nation, and who does so as much for the sake of *his ancestors* as for that of his contemporaries, reveals his spiritual orientation. So too do the

Warriors who discern in the cosmos the expression of *Logos* (Reason), or who affirm *the Tao* (the Way), reveal theirs.

In the next installment of this series, we will look at specific virtues prized by the Warrior—irrespective of when and where he has existed.

ESSAY 15

Guns and Self-Protection: Lessons from the Uvalde Shooting and its Political Aftermath

ALL TOO PREDICTABLY, the usual suspects spared not a moment to capitalize upon the recent school shooting in Uvalde, Texas for the advancement of their own political purposes. A few points:

First, the idea that it's possible to "stop" so-called "gun-violence," whether of the school shooting variety or of any other criminal sort, by simply passing but one more restriction on the distribution and ownership of guns—on top of the *thousands upon thousands* of such laws that already exist on the books—doesn't deserve to be dignified with a response.

To be clear: No remotely thoughtful person who is beyond adolescence can possibly believe this. The notion that mass shooters would be deterred by but another law nominally intended to accomplish what none of the other thousands of gun

81

laws have thus far been able to accomplish is the spawn of delusion and dishonesty. It is categorically unserious.

Second, the very term "gun-violence" is sophomoric. This is political rhetoric designed to advance an agenda. Politicians, their apologists in corporate media, and social activists know that if they say it often enough, the term "gun-violence" will mesmerize the masses into regarding the gun as possessing talismanic powers. "Gun-violence" is a crude anthropomorphism in that it personifies an inanimate object.

That it is only when guns are used for nefarious purposes, or by criminals, that the term "gun-violence" is employed is a further tip of the hat that the term is valued on account of its political expediency—and not for its accuracy. Are Russians and Ukrainians currently engaging in "gun-violence?" Are those law-abiding citizens and/or law enforcement officers who stop mass shooters and other criminals by shooting them engaged in "gun-violence?" Did the American soldiers who stormed the beaches of France on D-Day partake of "gun-violence?"

Automobiles and other objects are also used to commit violence, including homicidal violence. When, for example, a black male with a history of expressing anti-white animus drove his vehicle into a group of white people who were participating in a Christmas parade in Waukesha, Wisconsin, there were no cries—nor should there have been any cries—denouncing "car violence."

A tenet of Confucianism is known as "the Rectification of Names." The sage's point was that in order to know reality, we must strive to recognize things for what they are. Politicians and partisan media propagandists who evade reality by trading in labels that advance their ideological ends are not, and cannot be, interested in saving lives.

Third, it isn't only the advocates of "gun-control" who personify guns. Many of the most full-throated defenders of the Second Amendment, particularly those who own guns, tend to anthropomorphize the gun as well.

It's true that a gun *can* be a great equalizer. However, it's not true that a gun *is,* necessarily, a great equalizer. Like hammers, pliers, wrenches, screwdrivers, etc. the gun is a tool. Just as the possession of even the most enviable toolbox does not a carpenter make, neither does the possession of all of the guns in the world make the possessor into a dangerous person.

The gun is only as good, as effective, as the person wielding it. It's not a "magic wand." Being an excellent shot at the range or even while on sniper duty is one thing. Being able to shoot and kill under the duress and within the ever-changing dynamics of a *gun fight*—that's something else entirely.

Just as a person with a toolbox must practice to become a carpenter (or, at the very least, to become relatively handy in the use of his tools), so too is it the case that practice is necessary if one is to become handy with a gun for the purpose of self-protection. This practice, though, can't just be limited to shooting stationary targets so many times every so many months (or even multiple times per month). The gun, being an artificial weapon, is merely an extension of one's natural weaponry, one's body. More specifically, in that it is for the purpose of getting the jump on the villain or villains that one obtains a gun for the protection of oneself and those in one's care, the gun, in this context, is a function of *the efficiency with which one moves one's body.*

But—and this is critical—this maximal economy of bodily motion is itself the fruit of a training modality that *must* include psychological conditioning of a precise sort. The efficiency of physical movement upon which the student of self-protection should be focused is not efficiency for its own sake. The movement is animated by a goal that transcends mere matter insofar as it is centered in *the will.*

And this goal is nothing more and nothing less than the *annihilation* of the enemy: The more efficiently, the more smoothly or fluidly, a person moves, the more deceptively he moves, and the more deceptively he moves, the greater his chances of being able to disorient the sense of timing of bipedal predators just long enough to...*excise* them from the human species that they've betrayed by preying upon innocents.

This being the case, it should be clear as to why a self-protection training regimen must include the cultivation of a combative mindset. It must educate students of self-protection into the virtues of what, in the lexicon of Warrior Flow Combatives, are known as "Perfect Clarity," "Moral Certainty," and "Ruthless Intention."

Perfect Clarity: All doubt, confusion, and ambiguity dissolve as it becomes self-evident that there is but one course of action that must be taken: the incapacitation of the enemy at all costs.

Moral Certainty: This is the *conviction* in the *righteousness* of one's resolve to incapacitate the enemy at all costs.

Ruthless Intention: This is *the focusing of the will* to settle for nothing less than the incapacitation of the enemy at all costs.

The simple possession of a gun and/or the shooting of one's gun at ranges is no substitute for martial training, the training necessary to make oneself into a peerless combatant and, thus, a danger to the predators of our world. The gun can make one's job of dispatching bad guys easier, certainly. It is, however, just an instrument, a function of oneself—a fact of which far too many arms-bearers seem to lose sight.

Finally, whether the police acted dutifully or not in Uvalde is not, as far as present purposes are concerned, relevant. The painful fact of the matter is that the law enforcement response on that fateful day serves as a glaring illustration of something with which all adults should have long ago reconciled themselves: Grown men and women, particularly the "posterity" of the those who bequeathed to them the Second Amendment, must assume responsibility for their own protection.

Even had the Uvalde police arrived immediately upon having been notified of the shooting within the school, and even had they acted immediately, they would not have been able to prevent at least some lives from being taken precisely because *they were notified after the shooting had already begun.* The police are the cleanup crew. They arrive in minutes when microseconds count.

This, though, is always the case, and can't really but be the case.

The conclusion, then, to draw from all of this is that decent human beings must train to become a danger to the indecent. And to this end, it is imperative that they abandon the potentially deadly delusion that the gun is the be-all and end-all, the quick fix to challenges posed by guttersnipes to their safety and that of their loved ones.

There are no quick fixes. If one is serious about maximizing one's odds of securing the well-being of the decent, then one must *train*. Train physically and psychologically so that if one should ever find oneself in circumstances that demand a violent response then, at the proverbial flip of the switch, one can become...*merciless*—and turn the hunter into the hunted, the predator into prey.

At that juncture, and with this mindset, the gun, while making one's job easier, cleaner, is still just a utensil that one uses because it's available. But if it *wasn't* around, then a person who tirelessly trains to brutalize those who brutalize the innocent would still take care of business, either by using some other weapon—whether one with which he (or *she*) was armed in advance (a knife, a club, or a walking stick) or a makeshift weapon (a rock, a bottle, a piece of glass, dirt, a stick, or whatever flat, hard surfaces belong to the immediate environment within which the attack unfolds)—or by using his (or *her*) natural weaponry, their hands, elbows, arms, shoulders, legs, feet, head.

Jack's late father used to say that, as far as he was concerned, operating a car with an *automatic* transmission wasn't real *driving*. It was *steering*. In stark contrast, driving—which is a skill set— was achieved while learning to operate a car with a *manual* transmission. Jack's old man's characterization, while an oversimplification, is not an altogether inapt analogy to draw in connection with the subject of self-protection. After all, anyone who knows how to drive a stick shift knows how to operate an automatic. The converse, however, is not the case.

Similarly, and as we have been at pains to show, those who train to protect themselves with their natural weapons can protect themselves with whatever artificial weapons are placed into their hands. Because the converse is false, because those who only train in the use of guns (by shooting at stationary targets) do not train (physically or psychologically) to crucify the violent *by whatever means* necessary, they are that much less likely to be as adept in a gun *battle* as they may otherwise have been had they committed themselves to training in a genuine martial art, a real art of war (Any who doubt this should ask themselves why it is that the United States Marine Corps continues to require soldiers to train in hand-to-hand combat and bayonet fighting).

Don't fetishize the gun. Don't rely upon the police, or anyone, to do what you can and should do for yourself and whatever innocents are in your orbit: Treat with the utmost seriousness your right and obligation to protect yourself and your loved ones by training to become the stuff of the nightmares of the worst of the worst.

ESSAY 16

Tips for Combat-Readiness in a Hostile Political Environment

WE'LL GET TO the point:

We propose that, the current political climate being what it is, rather than engage partisan-activists who not only clearly aren't interested in civil debate but who are hostile and even known to act violently, decent people, including warriors, should keep their distance, when possible, while cultivating a very simple mindset:

> *Live and let live until and except for when you have to unleash the dogs of war in order to protect yourself and / or others from the violent.*

The only justification for aggressively getting into the space of anyone is to defend innocents from an imminent physical threat.

Period.

Jack Kerwick and Al Ridenhour

This being the case, all other times that one person invades, or group of persons invades, the space of others are nothing less than instances of unwarranted aggression.

Thus, if and when *anyone* invades the space of an otherwise peaceful person, that person has every reason to assume that the invader means to do him bodily harm.

And he has every moral right, then, to act on that assumption and neutralize the threat by whichever means necessary—and ask questions afterwards, as they say.

To be clear: As long as an individual is not initiating an attack against another, anyone who steps intimidatingly into his sphere of influence (within arm's reach, roughly) is no different than an intruder that enters his home. Morally speaking, the Castle doctrine applies, for just as a person is entitled to maim and/or kill a stranger that he finds roaming around his home in the middle of the night, so too is a person entitled to maim and/or kill an aggressor who intrudes upon his personal space. Intruders—who, by definition, have no right to the goods of life, limb, and property of those upon whom they intrude—mean to do harm.

They pose a threat. And a person, then, acts legitimately when he acts to incapacitate that threat—no matter what it takes.

We're not suggesting that the decent, peaceful, and law-abiding go into attack mode whenever and wherever some barely literate clown with a megaphone spouts insidious rhetoric. Just the opposite: Let people, whether demagogic politicians, virtue-signaling propagandists, street rabble, or even drunks outside the neighborhood bar, idiots at the mall, or difficult neighbors talk whatever shit they want to talk—as long as they do so from outside of your sphere of influence.

Let them be—until they cross that threshold, for while they may not realize it, that single step from the outer rim into your space gives rise to a totally new situation. The dynamic of their interaction with you has just changed dramatically, fundamentally. At that juncture, *they are in your home.*

Some intruders may mean only to intimidate. In fact, this is

88

typically (though not necessarily always) the case with the shit-talkers, for a person who really wanted a piece of another person's ass wouldn't waste time putting the other on notice as to what he plans on doing to him; he would just do it, and, theoretically, have that much of an easier time doing so given that the person attacked wouldn't know in advance the attacker's hostile intentions (Those who can, do. Those who can't talk shit). Still, a person threatened is not a mind-reader and has no obligation to hypothesize as to the true nature of an intruder's intentions.

A person accosted by an aggressor could be injured or killed—whether the aggressor *means* to critically injure or kill him or not.

For this reason, once that fateful step is taken by an intruder into the space of his potential victim, it must be the case that he stepped into a No-Go Zone, the Point of No Return.

And if there are multiple intruders, then all of them must be made to suffer the same fate.

Your average person doesn't see matters this way, unfortunately. This, however, is only because your average person has learned not to see things along these lines. He has learned to think that the State, i.e. the police, can protect him from the dangerous. He has also learned, whether he is consciously aware of this or not, to think that the loud, the obnoxious, the crass, the cruel, and the violent are invulnerable.

Overwhelmingly (though not invariably), the police are not protecting anyone from attacks. Rather they show up *after* the attack has occurred. And no one is invulnerable. No one. These are lies.

The good news is that because the average person *learned* to accept these lies as truths, he can *un*learn them—and *re*learn. He can radically repurpose his mind.

Training in a real self-defense combat system, not a so-called "combat *sport*," but a system designed to teach average folks in a reasonably short period of time how to successfully defend themselves from dangerous assailants will go a long way toward liberating the average person from his ignorance on these matters. It will facilitate his rebirth, endow him with the mindset that he needs in order to minimize his odds of falling victim to thugs. Until then, bear in mind:

1. Ultimately, you and you alone are responsible for your own protection, and that of your loved ones.

2. When you view others, irrespectively of their color or ethnicity, their size or strength, their religion or their politics, their athleticism or their physical aggression, their criminality or lack thereof, remind yourself that they are bound by the same anatomical and physiological constraints by which all human bodies are bound. Look at their skin, yes, but see past their color, their muscles, their tattoos, their scars, their bodily piercings, etc. and remind yourself that their flesh is just a veneer concealing blood, joints, bones, and vital organs.

Remind yourself, in other words, that just as you can bleed, be broken, injured, maimed, and killed, so too can they be made to suffer the same fate.

Remind yourself that just as they have learned how to be merciless, so too can you learn how to become merciless, if only toward those who are merciless toward innocents.

They are mere mortals, their bodies made of the same stuff as that which composes your own body.

Miyamoto Musashi, Japan's legendary Samurai warrior, said that from one thing, one can learn 10,000 things. Well, remember that if you know where a person is in relation to your body, and if you are close enough to touch that person, you are close enough to annihilate that person.

3. Avoid if at all possible all potentially dangerous encounters with vermin who aren't in the least interested in listening to reason. Start trouble with no one. *Agree* to *fight* with no one. Mind your own business.

Just take care of you and yours and...*train*. Train so that if and when the violent give you no choice, you will without hesitation go to that place, that place of no return—for the violent.

ESSAY 17

Martial Arts and Critical Thinking

MOST PEOPLE, FAILING to recognize it for the temporally and culturally-specific conceptual construct that it is, confuse the prevailing paradigm of reality, the conventional wisdom, for self-evident reality itself. This is just the way it is and has always been.

And this is because most people do not invest the time and energy, the proverbial blood, sweat, and tears, cultivating the intellectual virtues, the mental habits that are sowed during countless hours spent in the pursuit of knowledge.

Nor do most people nurture the moral excellence of *courage,* the courage to dare—the courage to *be,* come what may. Courage or fortitude is that trait needed to so much as consider just the very *possibility* that what the majority has been led to uncritically accept as unmediated reality is nothing of the kind. Courage is all that much more indispensable if one is to engage in the often lonely and painful process of *actually exposing* the illusions, lies, and flagrant contradictions of the conventional wisdom, for it most emphatically *is* a *lonely* road to travel.

Thinking is hard. It is *painful*.

And it is painful in more ways than one. Rather, it is painful in all possible ways in which it is possible for a human being to experience pain. Because the human-person is a unity of mind and body—because the mind is infused throughout the body, the latter being "the *subconscious* mind," as some neuroscientists refer to it—the development of one's critical thinking skill set can be as physically laborious as the development of those skills required for the perfection of athleticism in any other activity. Admittedly, critical thinking is not about to leave one saturated in perspiration, huffing and puffing, barely able to pull oneself up from a dojo floor, or burdened with muscle soreness. Yet the *mental* exhaustion that one experiences upon burning the midnight oil in study *is,* ultimately, *physical* exhaustion (just as physical exhaustion leads to mental exhaustion).

It is labor-intensive. This is also in part due to the fact that for as intelligent or otherwise analytically fit a person may be, if a person's efforts aim only to strengthen the conventional wisdom, he won't have to work nearly as diligently as one who is seeking to transcend it. If a person lacks the ability and/or the will to undermine that dominant collective conception of reality, then for however much time he spends thinking (writing, researching, discussing, and debating) about it, he will always and only ever be doing it on relatively flat land, so to speak. Sure, there may be some hills, but scarcely ever any mountains, that he will have to surmount.

The person, though, who dares to challenge the claims made on behalf of the Cave or the Matrix must *descend*. He must dig his way, as if with a spoon, straight through to the center of the Earth, as it were, so as to seize the roots of the worldview of his peers and upend it.

The figure who embarks upon this enterprise is, quite literally, a revolutionary. He is a revolutionary, though, in the sense in which the likes of Socrates, the Buddha, Lao Tzu, Jesus, Saint Paul, Galileo, and Copernicus were revolutionaries. Just as these great men would no more have thought to deny that there are continuities between dreams and waking reality, neither did they deny that there were continuities between the dream of the worldview *from which* they sought to liberate their contemporaries and the waking reality *into which* they sought to deliver them: The former, after all, is based upon the latter—even if it is a gross distortion of it (Lies, or at least the most convincing of lies, always contain some truth, after all).

The point, though, is that the critical thinker is a revolutionary in that he doesn't seek to reform or conserve the status quo but, rather, to supersede it. There are two ways to do this.

The first is an internal critique. A paradigm (theory, worldview, system, etc.) can endure internal tensions, apparent paradoxes, and/or subtle inconsistencies. It cannot survive fundamental contradictions. If it lacks the theoretical resources to resolve these, then it threatens to implode. The critical thinker is one who recognizes these contradictions. This part is easy (for *him*). What isn't so easy—what is extraordinarily exasperating—is discovering what a thankless task it is trying to draw others' attention to the logical chasms in whatever the Narrative happens to be.

It can be at once astonishing and discouraging for the critical thinker to learn that most people, however intelligent or erudite they may be with respect to other subjects, simply but sorely lack the very skills that he can all too easily take for granted. They don't think, and couldn't care less about thinking, critically when it comes to the pronouncements of those who they've been conditioned to regard as "the Experts." It's at this juncture that, for the sake of his own well-being, he must remind himself that critical thinking does indeed consist of *skills,* habits that, like all habits, must be developed and perfected over time.

Critical thinking, as was noted above, also demands

fortitude, for heterodoxy has never been known to receive a warm welcome from the orthodox.

The second way to revolutionize the Zeitgeist is to assume a *meta* view of it, to force its self-styled guardians (politicians, bureaucrats, media propagandists, corporate CEOs, academics, entertainment celebrities, ministers, doctors, gurus, comprehensively, its *Experts*) to defend the very presuppositions upon which it's grounded—to reveal, in other words, that it is, from start to finish, a tapestry of untruths, an artifact, a construct, a *matrix* designed to enrich its architects, the Experts, while mesmerizing the masses into thoughtless acquiescence.

This latter course of action is even more formidable than the former, though both require Herculean strength.

Critical thinking is, increasingly, a conspicuous rarity. Neither the overall culture nor the educational system, from kindergarten straight through to college, truly encourage it. Quite the contrary: The rhetorical homage that educators pay to the importance of individuality and free thinking is wildly at odds with the institutional practices that they promote, practices that are patently designed to apologize for whatever the status quo happens to be (The "politicization" of academia is so-called only because academia, to an undoubtedly greater degree than any other cultural institution, reinforces the political-social status quo by supplying it with its intellectual rationalizations).

One need not pursue a *formal* liberal arts education in order to acquire critical intelligence (in fact, nowadays, a formal liberal arts education, i.e. college, is all but certain to *preclude* the formation of critical intelligence!). One can, and should, study on one's own.

A real education makes available to its students those virtues of head and heart that the English schoolmaster and poet William Johnson Cory once identified in his characterization of a liberal arts education. Students, he said, "are not engaged so much in acquiring knowledge as in making *mental efforts under criticism*." In other words, education exists for the sake of "*developing arts and habits.*" These are "the habit of *attention,*" "the art of *expression,*" "the art of *assuming at a moment's notice a new intellectual position,*" "the art of *entering quickly into another person's thoughts,*" "the habit of *submitting to censure and refutation,*" "the art of indicating assent or dissent in *graduated terms,*" "the habit of regarding *minute points of accuracy,*" and "the art of working out *what is possible in a given time.*"

An education breeds "*taste, discrimination*" and "mental *courage* and mental *soberness.*"

And all of these "arts and habits" develop simultaneously with an ever-dawning "*self-knowledge*" that would have otherwise been impossible if not for the education delivered (italics added).

Critical thinking skills, then, are not limited simply to mastery of the rules and principles of logic. The critical thinker is not a logic-chopping machine. Rather, the arts and habits that he possesses enable him to *empathize* with others to a greater degree than would be thinkable had he never acquired these skills in the first place, for between the intellectual and character excellences there is less space than is commonly assumed. It was this insight that Hannah Arendt grasped when, upon observing the capital trial of Adolph Eichmann, architect of the Holocaust, she remarked upon his "*curious, but quite authentic, inability to think.*" This trait, she was quick to note, was by no means peculiar to Eichmann. Rather, it is shared by most people.

Between thinking and morality, she would then argue, there is an intimate relationship: Critical thinking, in supplying the critical thinker with some measure of immunity against irrationality, immunizes him against conforming to the thought(lessness) of the majority—and, with it, the cruelty, bigotry, and other evils to which the herd mentality all too often leads.

Thinking is hard. It's also necessary.

ESSAY 18

Martial Arts and Paradigms

MARTIAL ARTS AS War (MAW) and Martial Arts as Sport (MAS)—these are the two paradigms that, by and large, define the contemporary universe of the martial arts.

Now, it's true, of course, that the martial arts are assigned values that don't neatly fit into the binary scenario that I've framed. Some value the martial arts primarily (or maybe even exclusively) for their historical, aesthetic, or spiritual significance.

This point being well-taken, it nevertheless doesn't undercut the overall point that, at bottom, irrespective of the individual's *subjective* reason for training in a martial art, the training modality in question is, *objectively*, better suited for either MAW or MAS. Katas, for example, while valued by many for what may be perceived as their spiritual, aesthetic, and historical richness, can readily be incorporated within a training modality suited for MAS—but most certainly *not* one suited for MAW.

The bottom line is this: the martial arts world is inhabited by two kinds of people, those who conceive of the martial arts in terms of war and those who do not. The latter subscribe to what we refer to as MAS.

Logically one cannot simultaneously endorse MAW and MAS because to do so amounts to violating the Law of Excluded Middle, or the Law of Contradiction. For example, "MAW is true *and* MAS is true" translates to, "MAW *is* true *and* MAW is *not* true." The martial arts are warrior arts and they are not warrior arts. This proposition, however, is self-contradictory. It is *necessarily* false.

And it is illogical precisely because of the ontological status, the natures, of MAW and MAS, respectively. War and sport, it is intuitively obvious to all who have so much as the slightest familiarity with both, are ontologically incompatible because they are fundamentally different types of things. For example, the likes of Audi Murphy and Miyamoto Musashi would undoubtedly lose a sports match to the Muhammad Alis and Conor McGregors of the world, but the latter would lose their *lives* to the former *if* the milieu in question was not that of a competition but, rather, that of mortal combat.

These examples also illustrate the mutual *incommensurability* of MAW and MAS: Between the two paradigms there is no common measure.

Amongst philosophers, the notion of incommensurability is a controversial one, for it has been used—it has been abused—by some to suggest that truth itself is either relative or even non-existent. But this conclusion does not follow from the premise that the propositions peculiar to one frame of reference may not admit of translation into the language of another framework embodying a radically different vision.

While there is no common substantive standard shared by incommensurable paradigms, this emphatically does not mean that "truth is relative," there is no truth, or (what amounts to the same thing) that there is no rational way of evaluating the merits of the truth claims made by competing paradigms. Not at all.

While there is no shared *substantive* standard, there are indeed *formal* standards whose demands no theory, no proposition, no thought can resist.

The cannons of logic are unforgiving (however much contemporary academic philosophers may pretend otherwise).

So, in other words, if a paradigm lacks sufficient resources to resolve the very problems to which the paradigm itself gives rise, then it stands condemned by its own lights.

The Law of Excluded Middle allows for no other verdict.

The measure of success of a paradigm is its ability to surmount the very paradoxes that it generates. If, though, the paradoxes prove insuperable, then the paradigm reveals itself to be incoherent.

In light of this, we can now return to consider the paradigms of MAW and MAS. The latter, it shouldn't take us long to realize, is indeed incoherent.

Martial arts are not sport.

"Martial" means "of, or pertaining to, *war*." Yet this is not just a question of semantics.

Etymologically or denotatively, it's true that no matter how many terms are lifted from their natural home, the paradigm of MAW, and smuggled into the foreign land of MAS, such terms can never possess anything more than an *analogical* significance within this new universe of discourse.

However, even connotatively speaking it's the case that spectator and participant alike know all too well that the so-called "combat" sports, being sport, are designed to preclude serious injury, to say nothing of maiming and killing.

Such things, though, are of the essence of war.

Sports have all sorts of rules that exist for no other reason but to ensure that the games can continue. These, then, are restrictions meant to guarantee the safety of the contestants.

This is emphatically not the case with respect to war, the *raison d'etre* of which is the destruction of the enemy.

So, it's not that there is anything illogical or self-contradictory about any of the individual "combat" arts that comprise MAS. Rather, it's self-contradictory or incoherent to conceive of them as *martial* arts. Thus, it's self-contradictory to classify their participants as warriors.

Participants are undoubtedly athletic. They may very well be brave, just, and virtuous in any number of respects.

But they are not warriors, for they do not train for war, for potentially mortal combat with assailants the intention of whose actions is to end their lives.

This leaves us with the paradigm of MAW.

To put the point another way, martial arts are the warrior arts or they are nothing. Arts conventionally recognized as "martial" arts doubtless deliver a variety of benefits. Yet *martial* arts they are *not* as long as they disavow, whether in word and/or in their training modalities, the intrinsically martial character of the warrior arts.

Instructors who purport to teach a martial art *must* regard their students as soldiers who are about to enter the field of battle.

That it is the crux of a martial arts education to supply students with the ability and the resolve to annihilate the enemy does not mean that it consists of nothing else.

More exactly, it is precisely the unequivocal underscoring of this principal objective that seamlessly supplements the development of situational awareness and other behavioral characteristics that render dramatically less likely the odds that students will ever find themselves in situations where they would have to get violent with anyone.

For instance, it is precisely because students are trained to achieve mastery of lethal violence that they are that much more mindful of—they're more *skilled* at—avoiding circumstances that could legitimize their use of that kind of violence:

No bars, clubs, drinking parties with strangers, or hanging out in otherwise potentially troublesome environments.

No eye-fucking, chest-thumping, shit-talking, or dick-measuring.

Those who are trained to unleash unrelenting violence upon the violent are unassuming. They don't seek to draw attention to themselves and they aspire to be kind and friendly to others—even those who they sense are assholes but with whom they have to interact for whatever reasons.

Violence, in other words, is the last resort.

Yet when one must resort to it, then—like a nation that must resort to war—it's all or nothing. There is no point in attempting to harm a single hair on another person's head unless one's person, or the persons of one's loved ones, are endangered.

So, if violence is what is necessary to protect one and one's own from possible death, then the violence must be ruthless to guarantee that the threat is incapacitated, and incapacitated within as short a frame of time as possible to minimize the odds of innocents being harmed, or harmed any more than they have to be.

The violence must be ruthless.

And in order for an otherwise decent person to become ruthless, he or she must be trained to feel in the very marrow of his being that violence in the cause of self-protection is righteous.

It is a moral, an eminently moral enterprise. It is indeed a matter of survival. But it is not only a matter of survival. Bacteria and viruses aim to survive.

Human beings, when the choices of others have foreclosed all other courses of action, at long last go to war in order to achieve victory over the enemy.

Warriors don't regard life as an unqualified good, and don't value bare existence at all.

They wage war in order to live good lives, to flourish.

While MAW is the only paradigm of the martial arts, it nevertheless is the case that within it there are systems that contain incoherence. It is in light of the standards of MAW that these systems—so-called, "Reality-based Self-Defense" or "combatives" systems—reveal their flaws. They either incorporate into their training modalities methods and techniques that are more proper to sport, or they encourage attitudes into their students that not only have no place on the battlefield, but are all but guaranteed to get them harmed or killed.

It isn't that these systems must necessarily be discarded. They do, though, require revision.

ESSAY 19

Self-Protection and the Problem of Fetishizing "Techniques"

WHENEVER POLITICALLY-ORIENTED publications feature any articles on the issue of self-defense, they almost invariably pertain to the Second Amendment right of Americans to own *firearms*.

The more fundamental principle of self-protection embodied by the Second Amendment, however, is seldom addressed. Yet it should be.

It needs to be.

A reading of it that frames the Second Amendment *exclusively* in terms of guns fetishizes the proverbial cart without paying any attention whatsoever to the horse that pulls it. The gun is anything but the magic wand that popular culture and, unfortunately, far too many gun aficionados, make it out to be.

The gun is only as effective as the person wielding it.

The same goes for any and all "unarmed" techniques and

combinations of techniques upon which many martial/combatives arts systems are based.

An analogy makes the point: One can have the most enviable of tool boxes, yet regardless of how many state-of-the-art hammers, wrenches, pliers, and screwdrivers a person possesses, neither the possession of these tools nor the knowledge of how they work at the most rudimentary level suffice to make a person a carpenter.

As more than one commentator has noted, the era of modern philosophy differs from its ancient and medieval predecessors insofar as its representatives tended to be obsessed with discovering a "technique," as Michael Oakeshott referred to it, a *rule* or *principle*, framed as infallible, by which *absolute certainty* could be achieved. Rene Descartes, widely recognized as "the Father" of modern philosophy, is the exemplar par excellence of this orientation. Descartes, equating, as he did, knowledge (as opposed to mere opinion or belief) with absolute certainty, embarked upon a quest to land upon a technique that would guarantee knowledge so understood. He was confident that he did just this by way of his "*Cogito ergo sum*" ("I think, therefore I am"), for this indubitable truth embodied the criteria of "clarity and distinctness" that he would employ to differentiate ideas that are immune to doubt from those that were not.

Beyond the subdiscipline of epistemology to which Descartes mostly contributed, ethics and political philosophy in the modern era would also come to be dominated by this faith in technique. Locke's (and Lockean) "natural rights;" Rousseau's "General Will;" Kant's "Categorical Imperative;" and Bentham's and Mill's "Greatest Happiness" principle are all techniques that, if "applied," would always preclude error.

Nor did such influential critics of traditional Western philosophy like Karl Marx and the socialist theorists that he inspired avoid contracting this modern obsession with finding short cuts to absolute certainty. While Marx's theory centered in "history," his conception of history, his *philosophy* of history, was nevertheless unmistakably modern in that he replaced the infallible principles or rules of the philosophers who he critiqued with allegedly infallible historical *laws* that were no less designed to achieve absolute certainty.

It's not that there isn't a place for principles, rules, laws, comprehensively, *propositions,* that we're here calling "techniques." Quite the contrary, they are indispensable to human life. And all premodern philosophers (and others) knew this. This being said, pre-modern thinkers didn't make idols of technique. They recognized that techniques don't exist in advance of the way of life, the constellation of historically and culturally-specific traditions, that they are used to assess but, rather, are *abstractions* of that very way of life!

Pre-modern thinkers, in other words, realized that principles are the proverbial cliff notes to a much more complex, nuanced, open-textured tradition. Just as, for example, the cliff notes to *Robinson Crusoe* are utterly unintelligible unless and until they are recognized as the abridgement of a larger, more intricate text, so too do epistemological, ethical, and political-philosophical principles lose all intelligibility unless and until *they* are seen as the distillation of the traditions to which they belong.

This excursion into the history of philosophy provides the context within which both the present state of the Second Amendment debate and the world of the martial arts is to be understood. Interestingly, we can see that it isn't just philosophers over the last 400-500 years that have succumbed to the temptation to arrive at an infallible technique, a Rosetta Stone, that would essentially speak for itself and solve all of our problems. The singularity of focus upon guns reflects the tendency of those who are generally on the correct side to view this one particular weapon as if *it* is the infallible technique that all but guarantees the safety of its owner. The larger context, the types of physical and mental training, that render the gun-wielder a force to be reckoned with—and that make him *or her* a force to be reckoned with *irrespectively of whether a gun is involved or not*—

are out of mind.

And whether within the traditional martial arts or the various forms of what are generally known as "World War II Close Quarter Combatives," training is invariably training in the mastery of techniques.

To repeat the point above about intellectual techniques, it's not that techniques in the martial arts are somehow bad or undesirable. Far from it! It's impossible for a martial art system to exist without techniques. They're both necessary and quite desirable. The problem, rather, is the manner in which technique is taught. This problem, in turn, arises from the more fundamental problem of how technique is conceived.

Just as a rule, a principle, or a law derives its coherence from the larger tradition within which it arose and to which it belongs, so too does a strike, a combination of strikes, or any artifactual weapon (like a knife or a gun) derive *its* coherence—in the case of the fighting arts, its *effectiveness*—from the context to which *it* belongs. And this context consists of physics, human physiology, the *uniqueness* of each human body, and the psychology that is indispensable for victory in potentially mortal combat.

More will be said about all of this at a later time. Or, rather, as much that can be said about all of this will be said at a later time, for there is much that defies explicit articulation, though it can be felt, experienced.

Chuang Tzu relayed an account of an interaction between Duke Hwan and his servant, Phien, a wheelwright. When Phien learned that the Duke was reading a book that contained "the words of the sages," i.e. the words of men that have long since died, Phien replied that the Duke, then, was reading nothing more or less than "the dregs and sediments" of those "old men." The Duke, taking offense that a lowly wheelwright would presume to be dismissive of the wisest of men, told his servant that Phien would either defend his remarks or be put to death. Phien responded by referencing his own craft. "If the movements of my hand are neither (too) gentle nor (too) violent, the idea in my mind is realized." What's tricky, though, is that "I cannot tell (how to do this) by *word of mouth*," for "*there is a knack in it*," and "*I cannot teach the knack to my son, nor can my son learn it from me*" (emphases added).

Hence, the words of the sages read by the Duke are indeed "dregs and sediments" as the greater part of the wisdom that gave rise to those words cannot be imparted—particularly now that the sages are gone from the Earth.

So, too, is a gun, a knife, or any natural weapon a "dreg" or "sediment" as long as it is the object of exclusive focus, a technique taught in isolation from the context that birthed it and upon which it depends for its meaningfulness, its effective execution.

Perhaps this impulse to reduce a tool, a weapon (including one's *natural* weaponry) to an all but infallible technique isn't peculiar to the modern West. Miyamoto Musashi—another Taoist of a sort (a Zen Buddhist, to be exact) and a 17th century Japanese Samurai warrior—may have intended to speak to this phenomenon in his own place and time:

"You should not have any special fondness for a particular weapon, or anything else, for that matter. *Too much* is the same as not enough. *Without imitating anyone else*, you should have as much weaponry as suits *you*" (emphases added).

The way to martial mastery (to training so as to maximize one's odds of successfully protecting oneself and one's own, whether with an artificial weapon or a natural one) is *not* to be found in fetishizing the technique.

ESSAY 20

On an Art of War

THE VAST MAJORITY of human beings, irrespectively of their circumstances of place and time, uncritically embrace whatever the prevailing paradigm happens to be.

As long as "the Experts" inform (or *misinform*) them of X, they, without thinking twice, accept that X is indeed true.

Matters are no different within the universe of the martial arts.

However, lest critical thinking is brought to bear upon the martial arts by those aspiring to study them, the real-world consequences could be ruinous for practitioners.

Context is everything.

Unless an instructor, an educator, in any discipline, but particularly in a martial art, is aware of the totality of contextual considerations within which knowledge is imparted and acquired, he is sure to compromise, if not utterly fail, in his mission to attend to his students.

What is the context of training in a martial art?

1. Most fundamentally, the martial art instructor must be ever-mindful that a *martial* art is an art of *war*. It is a *warrior* art.

The mass commercialization of the martial arts; the rise in popularity of so-called "combat" sports; the litigiousness of contemporary (particularly Western) societies; and the pervasive belief among the populace that violence is only ever licit when deployed by the members of those selected classes of professionals (law enforcement officers and military personnel) authorized as such by the State—together these factors have rendered even many a martial artist forgetful of the character of a martial art. Others who may not have really forgotten act *as if* they have.

Nevertheless, while the times have changed, truth has not, and a genuine, as opposed to a nominal, martial art can no more divest itself of its essence as a warrior art and remain a genuine martial art than a square can divest *itself* of four sides and remain a square.

Connotatively speaking, anyone and everyone who aspires to train in a martial art does so with the expectation of learning what is commonly referred to as "*self-defense.*" In other words, everyone believes (and believes justly) that training in a martial art is training for the purposes of defense.

Hence, the martial arts, the warrior arts, are also the arts of defense.

What all of this means is that self-defense instructors must, first and most basically, labor tirelessly to help instill in their students both the ability and the resolve to *crush* those who would prey upon innocents.

To be certain, training in self-defense encompasses more than just the skill and the will to kill, to incapacitate aggressors by whichever means necessary. Situational awareness, for example, is key, for a heightened awareness of one's circumstances can dramatically diminish one's odds of ever having to engage violently with anyone. But self-defense training is nothing of the sort unless and until it has as its telos the ability and the willingness to, as founder of Warrior Flow Combatives and retired USMC Lieutenant-Colonel Al Ridenhour puts it, *"go big."*

Any self-styled self-defense instructor who doesn't feel this in the very marrow of his being and teach his students to feel likewise has no business being in the business.

2. Since those who seek out self-defense instructors do so in order to become as proficient as they can in the art of decimating assailants who threaten them and their own, this entails that their instructors know the difference between so-called "combat" sports, on the one hand, and, on the other, the nature of war, or what is typically known as "reality-based self-defense."

In knowing *this* difference, self-defense instructors are well aware of the fact that the training methodologies and modalities proper to any and all *sport* or contest-oriented activities have no place within the training schema of a warrior art, a self-defense system.

It's not, of course, that there can't be or aren't overlaps between some sports training methods or drills and those of the warrior arts. Yet such overlaps, owing to certain universal facts regarding human physiology and human psychology and to the fact that, to paraphrase Bruce Lee, a punch is just a punch and a kick just a kick, while inevitable, do not obviate the truth that the essence of a self-defense, combatives system and that of any sport are categorically incompatible with one another.

Actually, it's more accurate to say that the training modalities of the two are mutually *incommensurable*: The terms of the one can't be translated into those of the other.

Consider the conditions under which contestants in *all* "combat" sports engage one another, conditions that determine the shape of their training modalities.

They know:

a) they are contestants—not combatants;
b) at least months in advance, who exactly it is that they will compete against;
c) their rivals will be athletes comparable in all relevant physical respects to themselves;
d) they are required to wear protective gear designed to minimize the odds of seriously harming themselves and their opponents;
e) they are forbidden, by way of dozens of rules, from launching the kinds of strikes and kicks that are designed to critically injure, maim, and kill: Gouging the eyeballs of one's opponent, tearing his testicles, chopping or punching him in his throat, shattering his shin, snapping his neck, and crushing his skull by stomping upon it after he's down are all categorically prohibited;
f) there will be no use of weapons;
g) there will not be multiple attackers;
h) there will be referees to ensure that the rules are enforced;
i) the terrain on which they will engage is not made of concrete, much less cracked and uneven concrete with debris and broken glass;
j) they don't need to concern themselves with the elements, i.e. the weather, the temperature, and whether there's slick surfaces, from rain, snow, or ice, on which they could slide and fall;
k) they don't need to worry about wearing cumbersome attire;
l) they don't need to worry about having to engage their opponent in the dark, or in a club with a strobe light;
m) their match is limited in advance by a specific number of rounds, and that they will have time in between these rounds to recharge;

n) they needn't worry about being arrested for fighting.

This list of constraints that define the context of the "combat" sports is not meant to be exhaustive. What should be clear, however, is that not a single one of these conditions pertains to self-defense. This leads us to the next aspect of the contextual framework of the latter.

3. The average person who pursues self-defense is not a 20-something year old male athlete in prime physical condition. It is not uncommon for aspiring self-defense students to be middle aged (and older), and they include men and women who are only interested in learning to train in a way that will enable them to move in such a way that will compensate for whatever aches, pains, and injuries they've acquired over their lifetimes. No small number of those who enroll for self-defense training may have otherwise been living relatively sedentary lifestyles for decades before they enroll.

It's not just that they aren't especially athletic, and perhaps were never so. Neither are they bouncers, bodyguards, corrections officers, police officers, and military personnel.

Some may have never been in a fist fight. They may have never thrown a strike. Some may have never picked up a weight.

This observation is of critical importance for two reasons:

First, what it means is that self-defense students come not just in various body-*types*, but in *unique, individual bodies.* Moreover, the latter are glaringly different from those competing in the pugilistic sports.

Second, those instructors who have backgrounds in law enforcement, the military, "combat" sports, bouncing, etc. must grasp that *those very backgrounds of theirs* could *hinder* their effectiveness as instructors *if* they make the erroneous, but all too common, error of equating training in any of these areas with self-defense training, i.e. the self-defense training sought by civilians.

Just as sports training constitutes a radically different context from that of self-defense training, so too do those situated in these other areas find themselves in fundamentally different sorts of contexts than that within which the civilian who trains for self-defense finds him or *her*self.

Law enforcement officers and military personnel are agents of the State who, as such, are authorized to use violence against those whom the State deems deserving and within the legal qualifications, the "rules of engagement," that the State establishes: Their appropriation of violence is always and only ever limited by the nature and scope of the specific roles that they assume vis-à-vis the belligerents on whom they're expected to focus. Moreover, because these belligerents—criminal suspects, in the case of police officers; convicts, in the case of corrections officers; and enemy combatants, in the case of soldiers—know in advance the rights and duties of the State actors with whom they may have to reckon, the dynamics of the adversarial relationships that obtain between them is entirely different than the dynamic that obtains between a civilian and the scumbag that decides to prey upon him or her.

Implicit in each frame of reference are rules that are presupposed by both the good guys and the bad guys that operate within them: Police officers, corrections officers, and soldiers wear uniforms, and it is common knowledge that they carry weaponry of various sorts that they have the right and the obligation to wield if circumstances occasion it. This being said, police and corrections officers are expected to use only so much violence as is needed to *restrain* suspects and convicts, respectively. And soldiers, at least nowadays, while expected to win wars, are also forbidden from employing force deemed "excessive." Plus, militaries in the 21st century rely on bullets and bombs—two things that may not always be handy for the average civilian who trains in self-defense for the purpose of neutralizing, within a microsecond's notice, a violent threat on the streets or in his or her home. How one trains is how one fights.

Nor do bouncers or security forces, though hired by private employers, operate independently of the context that constitutes their own sphere of influence. Bouncers have a limited area that they are entrusted with surveying for the limited time that they are on the job, and they voluntarily assume the responsibility of minimizing conflict within the establishment by which they're hired for the sake of protecting customers from other customers and their employers from adverse legal repercussions.

The frame of incentives and constraints within which bouncers function, like the frames of incentives and constraints within which law enforcement officers, athletes, and military personnel function, is a dramatic different frame of incentives and constraints than that which a civilian inhabits.

All self-defense training must be predicated upon this.

Self-defense instructors *must know their students*.

4. Knowing their students means knowing that the average person who pursues self-defense training does so because they harbor *fears* generally and, specifically, the fear that they lack what it takes to rise to the task of defending themselves and their loved ones if the need to do so ever arises.

Self-defense training is fear-management. Self-defense instructors have a duty, therefore, to help their students surmount this fear.

Students seek self-empowerment. Thus, the emphasis on *survival* that has become the modus operandi of the reality-based self-defense world is misplaced, for it is *dis*empowering. Victims survive. Those seeking self-empowerment through self-defense training need to be encouraged to settle for nothing less than *victory* over whomever would make of themselves the enemy of God and humanity by preying upon them.

Far too many self-defense instructors disempower their students. Students' fears are enflamed by an excessive focus upon both the dangers posed by human predators *and* the legal consequences of defending oneself.

Are there dangerous, wicked people in the world? Of course! And no one on the planet needs *less* convincing of this than precisely those who enroll in a self-defense course! After all, it is this awareness that motivated them to want to train in self-defense in the first place. There's no harm in students being reminded from time-to-time of the evil among us, but there can indeed be great harm inflicted by self-defense instructors who insist upon romanticizing human vermin by endowing them with powers far exceeding those of mortal men.

The violent are no less mortal than anyone else.

Self-defense students should be encouraged to never forget that the smallest, weakest, slowest, and most peace-loving can, with proper physical and mental training, reduce to dust and ashes the biggest, strongest, fastest, and most brutal.

They should be habituated into believing, with impassioned conviction, that mobsters, gang-bangers, terrorists, and thugs of every sort are vulnerable entities, composites of blood, bones, and vital organs that, as such, bleed, break, suffer, and die.

This is the mindset that must be cultivated.

If the bad guys can become dangerous, so too can law-abiding, peaceful citizens train to become likewise.

In fact, self-defense instructors, given their obligation to empower their students, should spare no occasion to impress upon those in their charge that they can and *will* become *more* dangerous than the criminals who they now fear.

Students should be trained to transform themselves into the predators of those who would make the lethal error of preying upon them.

Again, while it is indeed important to know the laws on this matter, instructors shouldn't be excessive in lecturing their students on the need to avoid using violence except for when absolutely necessary. Self-defense students are the last people who are likely to use violence for any other reason—the *sole reason* for why they enrolled in a self-defense program in the first place!

These lectures aren't just superfluous. They are disempowering, stoke the flames of fear, and, because of all of this, could potentially bring a student to ruin if his or her life is on the line. The fear of legal reprisals could lodge into a student's mind and inhibit that student from taking the appropriate action at the precise moment that it is needed.

5. Finally, many self-defense instructors issue advice to their students that they themselves never admit to having followed themselves. For example, many advise their students to *run away*, if possible.

There's nothing objectionable about tactically retreating, for sure. But running may not be the best option, even if it is an option (can a woman with hip issues in her 60s run?). Not to mention, no one who invests the resources in time, energy, and money into a self-defense program needs to be told to run.

Never, though, can we recall having heard one self-defense instructor, particularly those with more visible profiles, relay any of the times that *they ran* from a situation.

Regrettably, there is a subtle, and not always so subtle, air of condescension that pervades the world of self-defense: instructors, rather than inspire their students to become every bit as skilled, and possibly more skilled, than the instructors themselves, instead present themselves as if they and they alone are the professionals.

Do as I say, not as I do, etc.

We reject this attitude.

ESSAY 21

Transforming into a Warrior

AT LEAST IN principle, it is common knowledge among martial artists of all varieties that the mental dimension of martial training is no less, and possibly a considerable deal more, essential than is that of the physical dimension (though, of course, vigorous, constant physical training is indispensable).

Warrior Flow recognizes that one's personality, one's very self, is constituted by one's thoughts, feelings, and actions. It is this constellation of the mental, emotional, and behavioral dimensions of one's self that is the lens through which one views the world, views reality.

So, one's identity is an intricate complex of these three aspects of one's being. You *are* your thoughts, emotions, and actions.

Given a lifetime of subconsciously wiring these mental, emotional, and behavioral habits into our bodies, we fail to recognize that, yes, they *are* habits! It only *seems* that we were *born* this way, that our mental, emotional, and behavioral patterns are the products of *nature.* The truth, however, is that they are only what has historically been referred to as "*second* nature." They are *learned* programs that, unbeknownst to ourselves, we have burnt into the *subconscious* over the span of years and years.

This is good news, for what it means is that if you do not like who you are, you no longer have to be that person. Since your patterns of thinking, feeling, and acting, however deeply wired into your nervous system they may be, are learned, then they can be *un*learned.

And you can learn *new* habits, thus making of yourself, quite literally, a *new self,* a new person.

This in turn means that you can become a *warrior.*

Before a person can transform from his old self to a new self, he must first commit to doing so. This commitment requires him to take stock of his old self. As Dr. Joe Dispenza puts it:

> To transform from the old self to a new self requires us to become conscious of all our unconscious [more accurately, subconscious] thoughts, automatic behaviors, routines, and emotional reactions that we've been conditioned into.
>
> To become conscious of any of these unconscious programs is the first initiation to change.[11]

Given the context of Warrior Flow, a person must, first and foremost, acknowledge his fears. He must acknowledge that it is his fearful old self that he has every intention of crucifying. Before he can create a new self, he must, simultaneously, slay the old self.

This project of recreation begins immediately. In fact, the initial decision to train in Warrior Flow in itself is the first blow of the chisel into the stone that will eventually become the

---

[11] https://drjoedispenza.com/blogs/dr-joe-s-blog/back-to-basics

sculpture of the new self. Like Michelangelo's angel who he claimed to have merely emancipated from the prison of the marble in which it was encased, so too is Warrior Flow training undertaken with an eye toward liberating the Warrior within from the cesspool of irrational fear that concealed it.

Students can start remaking themselves from day one. By growing in ever greater awareness of the mental, emotional, and behavioral habits of their old selves, they can also continually imagine their future new selves that they are forging in the present. Their imaginings, however, are *not* lofty fantasies, abstract ideals, or anything along these lines. Rather, in visualizing their future selves, they must also *visceralize* their future selves. They must not only see themselves and the new world or reality that they will inhabit; they must see, hear, taste, touch, and smell their future.

Practitioners of Neuro-Linguistic-Programming would say that Warrior Flow students, to unleash their inner Warrior and become the people who they want to become, must imagine their future selves in an *associated* way. They must *rehearse* their future selves in the present. They must *become* their future selves in every present act of the imagination.

They must think and feel as their future selves think and feel.

And, of course, they must act like their future selves (within reason, of course, for while envisioning and visceralizing one's future Warrior self, one must envision oneself waging war against enemies—actions, needless to say, in which one wants to avoid actually engaging if one isn't actually threatened by predators).

But one can begin to act like a warrior by training each and every day to become a warrior.

To repeat a point made above, the aspiring Warrior Flow student should understand in no uncertain terms that the transformation that he will undergo, and that he *must* undergo if he is to gain from his Warrior Flow training that which it exists to supply, is not *symbolic* or *figurative*. It is *literal*.

It is literal because neurologically, biologically, chemically, psychologically—in all of these respects the student transforms.

Again, Dispenza is helpful here as he explains the process by which a person can cease to be the person who he has been and become someone new:

> *Throughout the day, I review how I am doing and stay conscious. Via awareness combined with repetition, I fire and wire these new thoughts and behaviors into the fabric of my nervous system. In the act of combining the emotions of my future with my intentions, I am conditioning my body into a new future.*

Dispenza elaborates:

> *The more I perform this process, the more I systemically install **new circuitry** into my brain, while at the same time **chemically** and **genetically** conditioning my body to become that new personality.* [emphases added]

Dr. Dispenza notes that as you…

> *…rehearse these new ways of being and think about who you are going to be in your waking day…the more they become automatic, and it's that new automatic neurological network that creates a new level of mind.*

The brain "will look like you've already experienced that [envisioned, future] reality." Thus, these "mental rehearsals" have the effect of "priming the brain into a new future" as opposed to "revisiting the old circuitry from the past."

In short:

> *When you emotionally embrace your new life before it happens, you literally change your body's biology.*

The idea is that since "the environment signals the gene, and the end product of an experience in your environment is an emotion, you are signaling new genes *ahead of the environment*."

The conclusion is simple and straightforward:

> *Thus, because your body is so objective, it does not know the difference between the real-life experience that produces the emotion and the emotion you are creating without the real experience.*

To put this another way, as you begin to think, feel, and act differently, "you are becoming a different personality who is connected to a new personal reality."

Warrior Flow recognizes that this is how in fact people become new selves. Most people, though, have a difficult time wrapping their minds around any of this. Dispenza's explanation is as clear and concise as any, so it is worth once more quoting him:

> *To feel and experience the emotions of your future in the present moment—before that future has occurred—is what most people generally have a hard time with, because most people are waiting for some* **thing,** **person,** *or* **event** *to happen in their life to take away that feeling of emptiness, lack, or separation.*
> [all emphases added]

Most people are reactive.

They erroneously think that external agents and circumstances can rescue them.

The Warrior knows better.

He doesn't wait for his future to *happen* to him. He creates it, and relishes, in each present moment, in the process by which he creates it.

His future will materialize, but only if he creates it.

Even the most novice of Warrior Flow students, as soon as they proceed to rehearse their Warrior's future, begin, with the first rehearsal, to make that future a reality.

ESSAY 22

Focusing on What Matters in the Warrior Arts

LEGION IN THE martial arts community are those who spend no small measure of time in venues and on forums of various sorts debating over what, if any, is the *superior* art.

Superior, it's critical to grasp, is meant something like most conducive to *winning* against an *opponent* in a real street *fight*.

There are undoubtedly some skilled martial artists and seasoned street fighters who make insightful contributions to these conversations. Yet the fact that they would spend a fraction of a second paying this question the slightest thought exposes a profound, elementary flaw in their training—regardless of the art in which it is they happen to train.

Let's be blunt, for this topic is, quite literally, a matter of life or death:

The topic that commands the attention of these practitioners of the martial and pugilistic arts on their forums of choice is utterly irrelevant to the only question on which they *should* be focused. If they are instructors, they do their students a grave disservice by preoccupying themselves with *bullshit* concerning whose karate and Kung Fu is best.

"Martial" means of or pertaining to *war*. The martial arts, in their historical, truest sense, are the warrior arts. And warriors don't "fight" against "opponents" with an eye toward besting them.

Rather, that for which warriors train is nothing more and nothing less than the *annihilation* of the *enemy* from the land of the living.

Period.

So, the ultimate question, that to which all others must be subordinate, is this:

> *Does my training prepare me, at a millisecond's notice, to kill, unapologetically, with all of the brutal efficiency that the human imagination can conjure, any and all two-legged predators that wage war on the lawful?*

Implicitly, even if not explicitly, those who engage in talk regarding who can best who in a fight are subconsciously conditioning themselves for confrontations on the streets that they continue to conceive as analogous to sporting matches, the adult's version, say, of the proverbial schoolyard scrap. Nor can this subconscious conditioning be avoided, for as practitioners of Neuro-Linguistic-Programming (NLP) and other scientists have long established, the language we use shapes and reflects our beliefs, which in turn shape our behaviors, which in turn shape our language, and so forth and so on in a perpetual, self-reinforcing loop.

Hence, those who think in the terms of a sports lexicon will train for sport.

Many of the comments made during the course of these discussions regarding ground grappling, wrist locks, joint manipulations, arm bars, leg sweeps, pressure points, choke holds, and, in general, the virtual infallibility (to judge from their descriptions) of all MMA fighting, boxing, and wrestling techniques make this point in spades.

My thesis regarding the fundamental flaw in the training paradigm within which contributors operate is further supported by the experiences that they share.

They will recount, for example, confrontations in which they were involved that were preceded by either eye fucking, shit-talking, or any number of other signals that should've been spotted and addressed so that the confrontation could've been preempted. Or some will refer to the techniques that they applied to some "wise ass" or "tough guy" *after* the latter did or attempted to do something to them.

The problem here should be obvious: There is no "fighting" for students of the warrior arts. As veteran combat instructor Bradley Steiner memorably insisted: "Self-defense is *war* in microcosm."

It is worth considering two other quotations from Professor Steiner that are especially germane to the topic at hand:

> *Many who resort to violence at the first slight hint of what they think of as 'disrespect,' or a challenge to their manhood, or as a need to quickly beat someone—before he beats them, etc. do so because they are **not skilled enough** to feel the inner confidence that comes from being **genuinely prepared**.* [emphases added]

> *...in fact, it is the person who **lacks** skill and confidence in his abilities who is the most likely to become needlessly volatile, and get into avoidable encounters with others.* [emphasis original]

To further make the point, he once shared a quotation (by a Charley Reese) in his monthly newsletter that cut to the heart of the matter:

> *The truly dangerous man dresses inconspicuously and is soft-spoken. He walks away from most confrontations. The only time you learn that the truly dangerous man is mad at you is a split second before you die, for he **never fights**. He only **kills**. The truly dangerous man knows that fighting is what children do and killing is what men do.* [emphases added]

The only justification for real world violence is the protection of self and those innocents within the self's orbit against the aggressions of predators. And then—*then*—when violence is warranted, the use of that violence must be instantaneous, overwhelming, and at least potentially *homicidal*. Whether one thinks that the choice to kill the enemy is the best choice will depend upon one's intuitive assessment of the unique circumstances within which the confrontation unfolds. If, though, it *is* the best choice, then by all means the defender, the Warrior, should extinguish the enemy's existence without further ado.

And if there are multiple enemies? Then, under no uncertain terms, *all attackers must all die.*

The training modality of Warrior Flow Combatives is indeed unique among the warrior arts inasmuch as both its physical and, crucially, mental aspects, is predicated upon the assumption that self-defense is war and, thus, those who train for war train to become lethal warriors.

Students in Warrior Flow do not train to fight. They train to reduce predators to prey, to become the incarnation of the enemy's worst nightmares, to paralyze the enemy with the same terror that the enemy exists to induce in others. Students train so that, through sheer will, if and when they must, they can, in effect, nuke the enemy to kingdom come. And if they choose to spare his life, he will be forever haunted by the trauma that he suffered at their hands (and their arms, elbows, feet, legs, and/or whatever other extensions of their natural weapons with which they may opt to bludgeon him).

This is the mindset that Warrior Flow Combatives inculcates in students. It should be the mindset of all students of the martial arts.

Regretfully, those who are fixated upon determining who can kick whose ass in class, in a bar, or even on the streets, and who concern themselves with figuring out whether a guy who trains in Tae Kwon Do can beat a trained Mixed Martial Artist, a boxer, or a student of BJJ have not only got their priorities ass backwards. They are preventing themselves from becoming as good as they can be in order to prevail in the only "fight" that ultimately matters: the "fight" of and for their lives.

This oversight, needless to say, can get them killed. Worse, if they are instructors, their oversight can get *their students* killed.

It's almost incredible that any of this needs to be pointed out. Those who undertake any martial or pugilistic art do so because they believe that in so doing they will acquire the skills necessary to protect themselves against violent attackers. This being so, it should go without saying that to achieve this end, they must acquire the physical and psychological virtues necessary to go scorched Earth on the violent. If the art doesn't supply these skills, then it is not a genuine martial art, for unless one goes Hiroshima and Nagasaki on predators, predators will do just this to those upon whom they prey.

This is the governing philosophy of Warrior Flow Combatives. It restores the martial to the martial arts.

Focus on what matters.

ESSAY 23

Warrior Flow 9

A FRIEND, MARK, who is not any kind of martial artist, recently expressed a point of view that is all too common. It is treated as axiomatic by most people and even among the vast majority of martial artists and sports contestants.

The viewpoint is this:

Warriors, i.e. those who engage in potentially mortal combat, must be *athletic*, i.e. muscular, agile, quick, big, and strong. Presumably, then, warriors must be relatively young, and they must be men, for the young, generally speaking, are more athletic than the old and men, generally speaking, have all of these physical advantages over women.

It is unquestionably the case that, in a confrontation, power, size, and speed militate in favor of those who possess them over and against those who do not. Yet they are not the *decisive* advantages that Mark assumed them to be.

Of course, Mark is no different than the vast majority of

people who share his assumption.

There were still other presuppositions that Mark held. While referring to a childhood acquaintance of his who, at 40-ish, is now a Navy SEAL and in prime physical condition, he remarked that he would bet anything that on any day this guy who he has known for decades would "take" anyone in a "fight."

It became clear immediately that, understandably, Mark's thought is the product of a conventional paradigm that in turn has been shaped by a number of influences of which neither he nor most others who have imbibed it are aware.

Those who fail to see beyond this paradigm fail to grasp the insight around which the English philosopher Thomas Hobbes developed his whole philosophy way back in the 17th century:

> *Nature hath made men so equal, in the faculties of the body, and mind; as that though there be found one man sometimes manifestly stronger in body, or of quicker mind than another; yet when all is reckoned together, the difference between man, and man, is no so considerable, as that one man can thereupon claim to himself any benefit, to which another may not pretend, as well as he.*

Intellectually speaking, this means that there is actually considerable parity between men:

> *...for prudence, is but experience; which equal time, equally bestows on all men, in those things they equally apply themselves unto.*

When it comes to physical strength, Hobbes is blunt when declaring that *"the weakest has strength enough to kill the strongest."*

Those whose minds are locked within the conventional paradigm can't see what Hobbes knew because the very logic of the conventional paradigm precludes it. This paradigm derives from many sources:

1. **STATISM** Doubtless, the mystique that has been constructed around the State has brainwashed no generation as much as the present one into thinking that only commissioned State (government) actors—the "Experts"—can capably, legitimately use violence, and only ever in ways and against those targets that these same "Experts" deem proper.

Statism would be recognized as the cult of sorts that it is had the guardians of its orthodoxy not been as stupendously successful as they've in fact been at hypnotizing untold numbers of people into accepting its myths and dogmas (like its "Wolf-Sheep-Sheepdog" doctrine).

In short, Statism has conditioned people into thinking that it is impermissible and maybe even impossible for anyone who doesn't wear uniforms and symbols of State power to competently exercise violence against those who threaten them. Statism has habituated people into believing that unless one is an agent of the State, one cannot be a *warrior*.

2. **Fighting as SPORT** Statism has led to this second development. In the modern world, the "martial" (meaning of, or pertaining to, *war*) has been excised from the *martial* arts as training for *war* has given way to training for *competition* (whether in class, the gym, tournaments, matches, etc.).

In other words, the training modality of martial artists (along with that of boxers, wrestlers, etc.) is predicated upon a number of assumptions concerning their opponents and a host of other circumstances regarding their fights that they can count upon in advance:

a) Those who train in a martial or pugilistic sport know that they will square off against a single opponent;

b) They know their opponents' track record, their weight, height, reach, strengths, and weaknesses;

c) They know exactly the date, the time, and the place of their confrontations, and they know as well the kind of terrain on which they will transpire;

d) Regarding (c), they know specifically that they will fight in a well-lit ring and on a smooth, flat mat free of rocks, pot holes, curbs, broken glass, and all manner of other debris;

e) In knowing (d), they know that their matches will occur under room temperature and that they will not have to worry about rain, sleet, snow, hale, and so forth;

f) They know that their opponents will not be under the influence of mind-altering drugs;

g) They know that absolutely no (artificial) weapons will be permitted;

h) They know that they are forbidden from executing *dozens* of kinds of strikes and kicks that are simply too dangerous;

i) Concerning (h), they know that they are forbidden from *maiming and killing* their opponents.

All of these suppositions are conspicuously absent from the training modality of warriors, those who train for combat on the battlefield, yes, but as well those who train for the purpose of self-protection and the protection of innocents within their proximity who are preyed upon by violent criminals.

Yet Statist dogma permits citizens who it doesn't commission to use violence on its behalf opportunities to engage in violence as long as they do so within the constellation of safety regulations peculiar to sports or games.

3. **Misuse of the term "WARRIOR"** This should be sufficiently self-explanatory. The conjunction of (1) and

(2) has led to an indiscriminate use of the term "warrior" with respect to anyone who has been masterful in virtually any endeavor, whether physical in nature or not. Practitioners of combat *sports,* certainly, but as well weightlifters, those who partake of aerobic exercise, and even those who pray faithfully, survive cancer, and simply prevail over travails in their lives have all been referred to as "*warriors.*"

There is no small number of good things that can be said about such folks. And while a warrior should embody virtues that transcend those that make him a master of crushing into oblivion human predators, no one is a literal warrior who doesn't train to accomplish the latter.

Real warriors, in other words, train to kill the enemy. Inasmuch as the kinds of people listed above partake of no such training, they are not, strictly and literally speaking, warriors. This means that they are *not* warriors.

4. **Media ENTERTAINMENT** Tens and tens of thousands of hours of imbibing film, television, and video game depictions of violence have led most people into thinking that real world violence is as choreographed as any of these fictional fights. They've also led people into thinking that there is nothing in the least impractical about the *telegraphed* nature of the strikes involved in these confrontations.

The flashiness, the pizazz, the coolness of the male (and, with ever-increasing frequency, *female*) characters who thrill audiences with their theatrical moves have no counterparts in the real world. The sights of Hutus hacking to pieces with their machetes Tutsi men, women, and children; Islamic terrorists beheading on live television hostages who they have declared "infidels"; Imperial Japan burying Chinese captives up to their necks and then unleashing vicious dogs to eat their faces; gang rapists penetrating their victims with crude instruments in every bodily orifice before shooting them in their heads and setting their bodies on fire—there are many adjectives that we can think of to describe these acts of violence, but "flashy" and "cool" aren't among them.

Warriors train for real world violence, to defeat, to demolish these types of agents of wickedness, these human predators. And "cool" has got nothing to do with it.

As Warrior Flow founder Al Ridenhour puts it: "Cool will get you killed."

No one knows this truth better than warriors.

5. **Adolescent "FIGHTS"** Simply put, since a good number of boys have been in at least a fight or two, and since boys are especially susceptible to being impressed by images from the popular culture as to what a "fight" is supposed to be like, they've tended to fight in accordance with these images.

So, they call each other out and agree to meet in, say, the school playground. Upon meeting, they *square off*, they "put up their dukes," and then they proceed to take turns punching one another with their fists clenched. They will also undoubtedly attempt to block some of those punches. When one boy is down or otherwise gives up, the fight is usually over.

Long after some of these boys become adults, they continue to think that this is the template for a violent confrontation. Only now, it is no longer the school yard, but, say, the barroom.

Here's the truth: As far as violence is concerned, these men still think as boys. Their mentality continues to be that of an adolescent.

As someone once notably said, a warrior, "the truly dangerous man," "*never fights.*" No. "*He only kills,*" for the "truly dangerous man knows that fighting is what children do and killing is what men do" (emphases added).

This is the Warrior mindset. Any "fight" that is prefaced, or is able to be prefaced, by time spent eye-fucking, shit-talking, chest thumping, man-dancing, dick measuring, etc. is a fight that can be avoided. That more men do not avoid them reveals that, in a critical sense, they are not the men that they can or at least should be, for they are still thinking and behaving as boys.

At the very least, they are most emphatically not warriors, for a warrior is one who trains to regard fighting as the stuff of children. There are few people who a warrior could kill with greater ease than the loud-mouthed asshole, regardless of who he is or what kind of shape he is in, who gives away his intention to prove how tough he is. To the Warrior, though, this type of man-child is a clown who isn't worth a second's worth of his consideration.

The only time that violence is necessary is for when the innocent need to protect themselves against genuine human predators. And then, *then* it must be unrelenting and unapologetic. Unconditional victory, at which point the innocent is standing over the body or bodies of his or her attackers, must be the only goal.

While this is the goal, it doesn't mean that the Warrior can't throttle it back once he or she is convinced that the Enemy has been neutralized. The Warrior must have the will to go all of the way, but if he or she is satisfied that the threat has been immobilized without anyone dying, then by all means matters should end there.

The choice must be that of the Warrior's, however—and not that of the bad guy.

And anyone, with the proper training, can become the Warrior.

ESSAY 24

The Use of Evil Exemplars in Martial Training

THERE EXISTS ON YouTube a niche that, apparently, only ex-convicts and former career criminals of various sorts can fill.

All of these podcast hosts claim to have repented of their ways and assure their enamored audiences that their only reason for tirelessly regaling them with stories from *"The Life,"* as Michael Franzese and other ex-mobsters continue to refer to La Costra Nostra, is to warn them away from taking the dark path that they themselves had at one time taken.

Before proceeding, we should be clear that, as disciples of Christ, we commend and encourage all who strive to transform themselves from agents of evil to agents of good. It is always a cause for celebration whenever Satan loses one of his children to *the Light*.

The question, though, is this: Have these one-time malcontents *really* seen the Light?

From what we've been able to discern, many of these guys, at best, continue to convey mixed messages. Yes, they do indeed persist in romanticizing the criminal life—all while criticizing Hollywood and other media for supplying the public imagination with images or organized crime that *they say* aren't realistic.

The truth of the matter—and this is particularly the case with these mob turncoats (who, incredibly, swear that they aren't turncoats)—is that these guys are careful to capitalize on the popular conceptions of the Outlaw's life. They have much to gain, both economically and psychologically, from what they are doing:

The more popular their podcasts, the more they can monetize on it. The more violent are accounts of their past lives that they can crank out, the "tougher" and more important they can make themselves appear in both their own eyes and those of their enraptured viewers.

If, though, any of these guys are genuinely serious about having redeemed themselves, then they should categorically reject both their former selves and all of their former associates as the Godless demons that they had been.

Even if, as is often the case with respect to Mafioso and the members of organized crime generally, these criminals had limited their violence to their interactions with *one another,* there is no denying that they did in fact hurt lots of "civilians." We're not just referring to the billions of dollars that taxpayers had been made to cough up because of the mob's infiltration of otherwise legitimate industries but, on a more intimate level, to those legions of family men who were coerced into relinquishing a portion of the blood, sweat, and tears that they invested into building their small businesses to mobsters who made them an offer they couldn't refuse.

No *man*, no *real* man, would ever think about taking a penny from another man who had earned that penny.

No *man,* no *real* man, would associate with, much less describe as *good,* anyone who would take a penny from another man who had earned that penny.

No *man,* no *real* man, would be willing to engage in violence just because he felt "disrespected" or otherwise ass hurt by what he perceived as some sort of snub.

No *man,* no *real* man, would ever pose danger to those who simply want to mind their business and live their lives in peace.

This needs to be the message communicated in no uncertain terms by each and every single one of these former criminals who purport to have had their Come-to-Jesus moment. It is imperative that, in all humility, they confess that their conversion from a life of crime to the life that they now claim to lead was nothing less than a conversion from *adolescence* to *manhood.*

They were never tough because they were never strong. They ran with gangs, so they were overwhelmingly followers. Even gang leaders derive what power they possess from their followers: take away their followers and the gang leader, whether of a crime family or of a city street gang, isn't shit: his power vaporizes, for he needs them as much, if not more, as they need him. Simply put, these YouTubers had been, essentially, bullies. The life they led was predicated upon the fear of those who they victimized—who, not coincidentally, were always those who were correctly perceived as being more vulnerable than their victimizers.

No honor. No manliness. Godless. Evil.

All of this must be conceded. Contrition demands this. At any rate, it is a start.

While the typical consumers of this crime porn turn to it for the titillation that they receive from it, others *can* benefit from it if they approach it for the purpose of simply being reminded of the fact that there *are* dangerous people who live among us. Violent criminals are dangerous. They are snakes and wolves. Because most people are sheep, their sheepishness renders them either oblivious, often willfully so, to the snakes and wolves or else in awe of them. In either case, the sheep's fear of the snakes and wolves leaves them ill-prepared in the event that the predators decide to prey upon *them.*

However, some people (admittedly, not many) will exploit the fear porn for their own purposes. They can incorporate it into their own educational curriculum as they train, mentally and physically, to become, not a snake or a wolf, but a *lion*—a full-blooded carnivore that, despite its ravenous appetite for meat, will consume only other predators (like snakes and wolves).

The point, and one that to all martial artists and others who train in self-defense should be unmistakable, is this: The presence of evil, dangerous people in the world is the ultimate reason for why one trains. Or, more precisely, the ability to *remove* evil, dangerous people from the world is the supreme and sole aim of training in a genuine martial system.

This is Warrior Flow's philosophy.

All other reasons that can and have been given for training in a martial art come in a distant second place to the desire to be able to kill, with all of the ruthless efficiency that one can learn how to muster, any and all evil, dangerous people that threaten oneself, one's family, or other innocents who happen to be in one's presence.

Warrior Flow training begins with the presupposition that the enemy (whomever he or *she* may be) is stronger, faster, bigger, taller, more agile, younger, and more aggressive than the Warrior Flow student. Potentially anyone, the student is taught to assume, can "kick his (or her) ass" in a "fight." This is the orientation that informs the entire training modality of Warrior Flow. Why?

There is a method to the madness: As long as this is the fundamental operational assumption, then students train to neutralize all of those hypothetical advantages that the enemy possesses *before* they can become a problem. And students learn to do this by training, not for a "fight," for the sake, that is, of giving someone an ass-kicking, but for "the fight of their lives."

They learn how to neutralize the enemy's advantages by learning how to think and move in ways that will enable them to kill the enemy (or, if there are multiple attackers, the enem*ies*) before the enemy can kill them.

Victory or death: These are the only alternative outcomes of a violent confrontation that Warrior Flow students are trained to accept.

ESSAY 25

Reminders to Warriors and Bad Guys

OVER THE LAST few years, an industry of YouTube podcasts hosted by former mobsters and former criminals of every conceivable sort has emerged to advance the campaign to glorify thugs that Hollywood launched decades ago.

Thanks to YouTube and other online platforms, criminals, or ex-criminals, now have a greater range of opportunities to depict themselves as not just "tough guys," but guys who are tougher than the vast majority of other human beings, and particularly those ever-growing numbers of average Joes who subscribe to their channels.

Of course, every merchant selling their wares in this genre swear that they do not mean to glorify anything, that, in fact, they are supplying a public service announcement insofar as they are trying to deter younger people from following in the footsteps of those who have lived the outlaw's life.

Maybe there's some truth to this, for some. As for others,

not so much.

At any rate, though, if these guys *really* want to deter younger guys from pursuing a life of crime, then their messaging must be unambiguous. Thus far, from what we've been able to gather, their messaging is mixed, at best.

When they acknowledge that neither they nor anyone with whom they ever associated during their lives as criminals were *men*, i.e. males who were good, strong, true; when they concede that, as male members of the human species, they never mentally and emotionally advanced beyond being juvenile delinquents, that they pursued their own self-interests by way of the path of least resistance and at the cost of breaking the hearts of their wives, children, and parents—*then* their messaging will be clear.

So be it.

A virtue, though, of this genre of "true crime" is that it supplies those who are interested with constant reminders that dangerous two-legged creatures live among us. And it is this knowledge, and this knowledge alone, that motivates some men and women to train in self-protection.

Yet it isn't just their victims, but the dangerous criminals, and alleged former criminals, who style themselves "tough guys" because of their penchant for cruelty and their history of preying upon the weak, the outnumbered, and the intimidated who are also imperiled. They've drank their own bathwater, swallowed their own shit, and forgotten, if they ever knew, a life-or-death lesson: There's a place to which you can't go with either God or a certain kind of person, namely, the kind of person who trains in an art of war, like Warrior Flow Combatives."

Those who prey upon innocents are wicked. And, while it's not preached often enough nowadays, the truth is that God despises the wicked. This is established throughout the Bible.

Take Psalm 5:4-6, for example:

> *[God is] not a God who delights in wickedness; evil may not dwell in you. The boastful shall not stand before your*

eyes; you hate all evildoers. You destroy those who speak lies; the LORD abhors the bloodthirsty and deceitful man.

Then there's Psalm 11:5:

The wicked, those who love violence, he [God] hates with a passion.

We could go on. The point: God detests the evil and promises, from the book of Genesis through to that of Revelation, that He will guarantee that the evil ultimately receive their just desserts—death.

The bad guys—as well as far too many others who aren't bad guys, including those who train in martial arts—forget, in other words, that the bad guys are mere mortals. Because they are mortal, they can be injured. They can be crippled, tortured, raped, and terrorized.

They can be killed.

In short, all of the unimaginably brutal things that they can and, in some instances, have done to others can be done to them—and not, necessarily, just by other career criminal vermin.

This last idea needs to be underscored, for most people, especially bad guys, apparently forget that one needn't be a criminal—one can be thoroughly contemptuous toward criminals—to kill a person with only slightly more effort than is required to extend one's hand and touch that person.

If a person can bleed from a paper cut, then he can bleed *to death* courtesy of another mortal.

As a human being, the most dangerous, violent low-life predator on the planet is, essentially (even if relatively speaking), as anatomically and physiologically restricted as is the most frail and timid of elderly women. This brute fact means that the elderly woman could drop his miserable ass under the correct circumstances—particularly if she *trains*, as the predator, like all criminal predators, has trained all of his life, to become a killer when she needs to become one.

The criminals are mortals, like you and I. They are bound by the same laws of physics and human physiology that bind the rest of us. What fundamentally distinguishes the criminal predator from otherwise decent people is that the latter have scruples that the former lacks. Predators have a ruthlessness that gives them an edge over those upon whom they would prey.

The good news, however, is that this ruthlessness is, overwhelmingly, learned. It wasn't learned through any kind of formal training, true, but, by virtue of a lifetime's worth of cultivating vicious habits, it was learned all of the same. What this in turn means is that if criminals can learn how to be ruthless, so too can decent folks. Only in the case of the decent who seek out competent instructors to teach them how to be ruthless, their ruthlessness will not be a vice but, rather, a virtue—a *martial* virtue.

It will be a character excellence, the excellence of a *warrior*, for unlike scumbags who are merciless toward unsuspecting, innocent people who they regard as nothing more or less than a resource, the decent who train to become ruthless train to become merciless only toward the wicked, toward those who imminently threaten them, their loved ones, or other innocents in their presence.

Warrior Flow seeks to make *good* people by making them into *dangerous* people—dangerous for criminals who may have otherwise preyed upon them. It aspires to do this by instilling in students "Ruthless Intention." Speaking to this virtue, Mushashi memorably stated that the martial student is to "attack with a feeling of constantly crushing the enemy, from first to last."

God has supplied all of us with everything we need to protect ourselves against the designs of the evil. Musashi made this point as well:

There is nothing outside of yourself that can ever enable

143

you to get better, stronger, richer, quicker, or smarter. Everything is within. Everything exists. Seek nothing outside of yourself.

The training modality of Warrior Flow is predicated upon this truth. Jordan Peterson shared a brilliant insight during an exchange with former Navy SEAL Jocko Willink when he said that a "*good* man must be a *dangerous* man." [emphases added]

To be good, a person must become dangerous, for the world is full of those who are dangerous but evil.

ESSAY 26

The Principles of Warrior Flow

IN KEEPING WITH the identity of the human person as an indissoluble unity of body and mind, the combative principles of Warrior Flow—**Equilibrium-Control, Subtle Muscle-Control, Perceptual Awareness, Dynamic Coordination**, and **Creativity**—supplies to students both and at once the physical *and* mental conditioning in the absence of which martial development is impossible.

Mastery of these five principles is tantamount to perfection of the three inseparable cardinal mental habits of **Perfect Clarity, Moral Certainty**, and **Ruthless Intention**. These traits, it's critical to note, are indeed *psychological* in nature. Yet they aren't *only* psychological. They are as well *intellectual*.

The psyche consists of the totality of mental phenomena pleasant and unpleasant, good and bad, rational, irrational, and even neurotic. The psyche is what it is. Its condition, in other words, is *descriptive*. The intellect, in contrast, is *normative*, for the coin in which it trades is *reason*. The intellect, that is, is supposed to be governed by *logical*, and not illogical, considerations. It always aspires to think as it *ought,* as it *should.*

In theory, the psychological and the intellectual are separate provinces of the mind. Indeed, in practice, for most people, the two remain distinct. Within Warrior Flow, however, the psychological and the intellectual fuse into one seamless mind. More accurately, they fuse into one seamless *will,* the Warrior's will.

The Warrior's will is nothing more or less than the considered determination to obliterate, at a microsecond's notice and without a scintilla of guilt or regret, anyone who preys upon innocents—whether himself, his loved ones and neighbors, or others—that are within the Warrior's presence.

Notice, the will of the Warrior is not the function of impulse, instinct, or raw passion (like fear or rage). It is a *considered* determination. It is the product of *education*, of training. Warrior Flow students are not only taught to always bear in mind that there are human beings in the world who are bigger, stronger, faster, more agile, more athletic, younger, and more dangerous than themselves. Their training is *predicated upon the operational assumption that anyone and everyone against whom they may battle has every one of these physical advantages over them.* The reason for this is simple:

When it is assumed that any and all potential adversaries are superior in every conceivable respect to oneself, then one trains so as to *neutralize* these advantages before they can materialize.

And Warrior Flow students train to neutralize the enemy *not* by focusing upon the mastery of any specific set of *techniques*, but by immersing themselves in the combative *principles* of the art.

The distinction within the context of self-protection between "techniques" and "principles" is essentially the same distinction between *"plans"* and *"planning"* that General Eisenhower once drew. "In preparing for battle," Ike remarked, "I have always found that plans are useless, but planning is indispensable."

The principles of Warrior Flow constitute planning.

With all due respect to their practitioners, we do not mean to suggest that the techniques of other arts these are "useless," as Eisenhower described plans. But, ultimately, training in principles is superior, for principles, transcending as they do all techniques, enable students to avail themselves, at a moment's notice, of possibilities for action to which a person limited to the techniques in which he has been trained must remain oblivious. The person who trains in principles, though, is ceaselessly planning.

In other words, Warrior Flow is a *system,* a *genuine* system.

It is not a buffet of combative techniques (that are, by and large, common to all self-styled combative "systems") *conjoined with* a method by which practitioners can condition their psyches for battle. There is nothing systematic about a salad—even though, between its ingredients, there may be a "family resemblance," to borrow the philosopher Ludwig Wittgenstein's term for things that, while similar, are not related by any common denominator.

Warrior Flow is not a Many that remain a Many in reality, but is only made to *seem* like a One via clever labeling.

Warrior Flow is a Many that is *really* One, a single, unified martial system. Its combative principles are conceptually or theoretically distinct but, in practice, essentially one and the same. Students don't—and can't—focus on anyone of the five combative principles while failing to master the other four, and since the movement that they are always seeking to refine through immersion in these principles is movement designed to decimate, with ruthless efficiency, those who would victimize innocents, it is equally impossible for them to engage in physical training without also developing the mental virtues of Perfect Clarity, Moral Certainty, and Ruthless Intention.

Warrior Flow is like an organism, not a machine, a constitution, not a collection. Unlike many other styles, it recognizes that since the numerous members of one's body are continually operating simultaneously, so too do these members continue to operate the same when they are engaged for the purposes of battle. Thus, Warrior Flow's training modality, as by now should be clear, is purposed for the sake of training students how to crush the enemy within "**the *Quantum* Sphere**," a spatial-temporal order comprised of *dimensions*—not sequentially or chronologically-layered events or levels—between which students are trained to "*tunnel*" or "*teleport*" and all with an eye toward destroying the enemy.

These dimensions are the three that human beings occupy in space, those of **Length**, **Width**, and **Height**. Yet they also include **Time**, **The Future**, **Anticipation**, and **Creativity**.

Time: A physical confrontation between two or more people doesn't occur only within space. We must remember that it as well occurs over time. And since time is relative to the observer, this means that victory over the enemy demands, necessarily, that the victor disorients the enemy by manipulating his perception of time, no less than his space-in-time.

For this reason, Warrior Flow students learn, through mastery of the five combative principles, how to always move *deceptively*. **Deception**, after all, is the basis of all warfare, as Sun Tzu declared. In moving with maximal economy, Warrior Flow students conceal their intention(s) from the enemy and, in so doing, radically upset his timing.

Through continual refinement of their subtle muscle-control and perceptual awareness, students learn not just how and when to *accelerate*, but, critically, how and when to *decelerate*. Via the development of the latter skill, Warrior Flow students become capable of both "*stopping time*" and "*slowing down time*" within microseconds—just long enough to send the enemy off to his eternal deserts.

The Future: "Fighting in the Future," to be more exact. "In battle, if you make your opponent flinch, you have already won," as Musashi noted. Warrior Flow students capitalize on this pearl of wisdom by figuring out quickly that in putting the enemy on the defensive, they force a response from him. What this in turn means is that in going on the offensive, they will lead the enemy to that future location at which they are already waiting, that juncture in time at which the enemy hasn't yet arrived but to which he is inexorably moving and at which his fate will be sealed.

It doesn't take any training for anyone to realize that by making any kind of movement toward another person, the person who initiates the movement makes the second move in turn. Effortlessly and without intention, we both provoke reactions from and react to the movements of strangers on a virtually daily basis (whenever and wherever we have to navigate space-time vis-à-vis other human beings). This being the case, Warrior Flow students train to learn how to provoke the kinds of reactions from the enemy that are designed to lead him to his own demise.

Anticipation: This is anticipation of *possibilities and probabilities,* of potential futures, potential ways within which Warrior Flow practitioners defeat the enemy.

In moving deceptively—i.e. with maximal efficiency, meaning no more and no less than one needs to move—Warrior Flow students upset the enemy's timing. What this means is that with each passing microsecond students dramatically *narrow* the enemy's range of possible courses of action while dramatically *expanding* the range of possibilities for themselves.

And this, of course, is all due to the fact that Warrior Flow students train to "fight in the future," that place along the space-time continuum where all of the possibilities of which they can avail themselves already exist and whose actualization they can bring about at a millisecond's notice if only they choose to do so.

Moreover, because they are in the future awaiting the arrival of the enemy with all of the patience—and eagerness—with which a batter awaits the arrival of the ball that he plans upon smashing, *whichever* possible future Warrior Flow students decide to realize is *correct*: Critical injury, maiming, and killing— whichever fate Warrior Flow students choose to allot to the enemy are in the cards for him, for the enemy is too far behind in time to do anything to thwart his own demise.

Creativity: It was mentioned above that Warrior Flow training simultaneously develops both body and mind (for the two are one), and that the mental aspect is psychological, yes, but as well intellectual. Here we should note that the intellect always involves *imagination.* Indeed, the imagination is integral to the intellect (even though the contemporary fetishizing of "Science" and the poverty of imagination of those who do the fetishizing have led many astray into thinking otherwise).

Warrior Flow training expands its students' imaginative capacities. It expands their conceptual horizons, revealing a virtual cosmos of possibilities and probabilities from which to choose in visiting destruction upon the enemy. By now it should be clear that Warrior Flow training equips students with this insight by enabling them to time their movement so as to teleport to the future—*their* future(s), the future(s) of their choosing—ahead of the enemy.

These are the seven dimensions of combat. Warrior Flow students train to battle in the Quantum Sphere. In so doing, they are always making themselves both **unavailable** and **unavoidable** with respect to the enemy. Moving, as they do, ahead of the enemy's movement, they are unavailable. However, they are also now unavoidable to him, for, being in the future, there is virtually nothing that he can do to escape the brutality to which he will be subjected.

This is Warrior Flow.

ESSAY 27

The Metaphysics and Philosophy of Knowledge of Warrior Flow

WARRIOR FLOW COMBATIVES is a genuine martial *system*. Its combative principles constitute a seamless whole that at once develops the mental and physical dimensions of the human-person.

Ontology

The human-person is a spiritual oneness—most certainly not some kind of disembodied soul of the kind conceived by Neo-Platonists, Gnostics, and Cartesians. In contrast, Warrior Flow's is an *incarnational* ontology inasmuch as the person is recognized as an indissoluble unity of mind and body. Just as, according to the Christian perspective, Christ, the Second Person of the Triune God, did not *inhabit* but, rather, *assumed* the human body of Jesus of Nazareth, so too does Warrior Flow suppose that

each and every person is a fusion of spirit and body.
Thus, training must begin and end with the person as he actually
is.

Epistemology

This incarnational ontology is inseparable from the epistemology
based upon it. As far as it goes, it's not inaccurate to refer to this
theory of knowledge as a form of *"empiricism"* (the position that
knowledge derives from experience). Yet this label only goes so
far, for since the advent of the modern era, empiricists—
motivated, as they have been, to counter their rationalist rivals—
have been all but obsessed with debunking innate and other
species of a priori knowledge.

Because its representatives were driven by a set of
philosophical and historical considerations peculiar to the cultural
milieu within which they operated, empiricism in its early
modern and Enlightenment guises was dogmatic. The
"empiricism" underlying Warrior Flow is more akin to that of
Aristotle (who was also a rationalist of a sort) than to that of John
Locke.

So, while affirming the experiential essence of learning,
Warrior Flow repudiates as the nonsense that it is Locke's fiction
of a *tabula rasa:* Locke's doctrine that the mind is a blank slate
prior to experience is of a piece of the same load of bullshit as that
peddled by his rationalist boogeyman, Descartes, who said that
the mind and the body are two fundamentally distinct
"substances."

The 17th century Japanese Samurai Miyamoto Musashi was
more on the mark:

> [T]here is nothing outside of yourself that can ever
> enable you to get better, stronger, richer, quicker, or
> smarter. Everything is within. Everything exists. Seek
> nothing outside of yourself.

Warrior Flow seconds this. This is why Warrior Flow instructors are really *educators* in the literal, etymological sense of the term. In the original Latin, the educator is one who "leads forth," who "takes out," who "raises up," and "erects." The educator *educes,* i.e. he summons to the heights of explicit consciousness the knowledge that the student, however inchoately or otherwise subconsciously, already possesses.

Philosophy of Learning

Warrior Flow has an overall philosophy of learning. Yet it also appreciates how this philosophy assumes flesh, so to speak, within the specific circumstances in which an aspiring student of the martial arts finds him or herself.

Learning, first and most fundamentally, is not limited to formal education. This much should be obvious. Human beings are always learning, and they are learning by way of doing, by continuously interacting with the ever-fluctuating environments by which they are affected and which in turn they affect. Yes, the subject/object distinction that has vexed philosophers for the last 400 or so years is resolved in practice every moment of everyday as people contribute to the creation of the very environment that constitutes (at least partially) their very identity. Between self and "non-self" there exists an intrinsically synergistic, a dialectical, relationship.

Learning doesn't always produce knowledge—if, that is, the object of knowledge is necessarily truth: People learn lies. They learn misinformation. They learn wickedness.

The goal of learning, clearly, is the securement of knowledge, and Warrior Flow is meant to provide students with knowledge of how to crush—logically, how to kill—those who, God forbid, would imperil them or theirs.

So, this is the first thing that any prospective student of Warrior Flow must know before he or she so much as considers the mere possibility of becoming an actual student. It is the first thing that must be unequivocally stated by any self-styled "self-defense" instructor of *any system*. Anything less is not just false advertising, but insidious false advertising inasmuch as it at once deprives people of a return on their investment (their money, hopes, energy, time) *and* potentially endangers them.

As a martial or combative system, Warrior Flow exists for no other sake than that of helping its students liberate from the layers of the lifetime of psychological and emotional garbage under which it's buried the Warrior that lies within them.

Nor is there anything hyperbolic, sensationalistic, or otherwise figurative about its use of "warrior" talk. A real-world physical attack against a person is tantamount to an act of war inasmuch as such attacks can and have resulted in those against whom they are initiated being critically injured, paralyzed, tortured, raped, and killed. For this reason, the predator who sets his sights upon innocents marks himself as, not an *opponent*—this is not a sports-competition or game—but *the enemy*.

Musashi:

> *The only reason a warrior is alive is to fight, and the only reason a warrior fights is to win.*

People process information through the cognitive categories, the conceptual lens, that have been indelibly shaped by the experiences that they've endure. So whatever information educators provide to their students should always be framed in a way that accommodates this fact (even if, ultimately, in order to discombobulate, maybe to even revolutionize, their students' standards and expectations). This is all of especial critical importance in the case of aspiring martial arts students.

Those who seek out instruction in the warrior arts do so in order to manage their *fears*. This is most fundamental. There is a variety of other benefits that can be reaped from the study of this subject, but, in the final analysis, there can be no doubt that those who train in a martial art do so in order to own their fear.

This in turn means that the last thing they need is for their instructors to reinforce the very fears that drove them to seek out these instructors in the first place. Yet this, unfortunately, is what occurs all too often.

For example, within some systems it is not at all uncommon for instructors to fill the already fevered imaginations of their students with tales and images of "prison-trained monsters," massively muscular, super powerful, tatted-up, hardened convicts that are all but bullet-proof. There is more than one problem with this:

1. That big, strong, predators exist is true, of course. However, the odds of the average person encountering one are miniscule to the point of being nonexistent;

2. One needn't fit the profile of the "prison-trained monster" in order to be a psychopath or otherwise predatory and, in fact, the overwhelming majority of sadistic bipeds do *not* fit this profile;

The biggest problem with this approach, though, is that it has great potential to *exacerbate* students' fears.

In other words, there is no need to belabor, and even less need to embellish upon, the brute fact that there are venomous scumbags on the planet. There is no need to adopt this approach when interacting with people, most of whom are already adults, who have already embarked upon the study of a combat art. They already know about the dangers that exist. If they didn't, they never would have decided to pursue martial development.

Thus, any system worth its salt will focus upon reminding its students at every turn, if not always in word, then during training, that the monsters among us, even if not human in the normative sense of that term, are nevertheless members of the homo sapiens species like anyone else.

This means that they are *mortal*.

They *bleed*.

And break.

And suffer.

And die.

If the most sociopathic, psychopathic "prison-trained monster" in the world can be touched, and touched even by the smallest and feeblest of elderly women, he can be *killed*.

And killed by *her*.

There are no supermen here. No one is invulnerable.

Self-styled martial or combat instructors need to fill their students' heads with, not just the *thought*, but the *conviction*, that he or she can become—no, is already *becoming*—the stuff of the nightmares of the worst of the worst. If a person can learn one thing, he or she can learn another. If a person can learn how to become a "prison-trained monster," say, then another person can learn how to become sufficiently ruthless so as to remove, without a second's hesitation and with all of the brutality imaginable, such a monster who attacks him or her from the land of the living.

The message needs to be—and this is what it only ever is within Warrior Flow—that in the real world, invincibility is reserved only for God. The bad guys are susceptible to every conceivable agony that they reserve for their targets. And this is bad news, this is terrible news for *them* if they victimize an otherwise law-abiding, peace-seeking student of Warrior Flow who some villains think are easy marks.

Yeah, there are evil, dangerous people on Earth. Well, isn't that the whole fucking point of training in a system of combat? Why continually harp upon it? Within Warrior Flow, this is the *problem* that doesn't need to be stated. Each and every self-protection system that purports to be anything of the sort is predicated upon it. The *solution* that Warrior Flow prescribes—that it embodies—is its focus, and the solution is to make as many *good* people *more dangerous* than are the evil.

Problem. Solved.

Most fundamentally, then, self-protection instructors need to know the psychology of their students. They need to know that successful teaching is a matter of accommodating the psychological needs and desires of their students, for the information that they supply is inevitably going to be filtered in terms of these needs and desires. And this, in turn, means that *what* is said and *how* it is framed will make all of the difference between whether a student succeeds or fails—both as a student and, potentially, in real life where the difference could be one between life or death.

ESSAY 28

Self-Protection Begins at Home

IT IS NOT uncommon for those who either read our work or who have consulted us about training with us to admonish us for daring to use the "k" word ("killing") while discussing, of all things, *guns*, the *martial arts,* and *the protection of innocents from human predators*!

Let's cut the bullshit: While a gun doesn't necessarily have to be used to kill an attacker, guns are, essentially, *killing* machines. *This is why they exist.* This is why millions and millions of Americans, to say nothing of the police, security, and military forces of the world, arm themselves with guns. And it's precisely because everyone knows this that the gun-grabbers know that they can plausibly (even if irrationally and unjustifiably) use this common knowledge as a pretext upon which to make it exceedingly difficult for Americans to exercise their Second Amendment rights.

So, those who own guns but clutch their pearls whenever

they hear someone talk about the need for good people to train to kill bad people are either hypocrites or genuinely confused. Hopefully, for the sake of themselves and their loved ones, they're just hypocrites, for hypocrisy won't necessarily prevent them from preparing themselves (physically and mentally) to incapacitate an attacker at all costs. If they are confused, however, lacking the will to do what they must in the event that they or those close to them are imminently threatened, then they render themselves and those in their care vulnerable to the predations of aggressors who share none of their reservations.

Their squeamishness is not just a harmless idiosyncrasy. It is a psychological adhesion, a mental knot that cost precious moments, even if just milliseconds, that could mean all of the difference as to whether the decent and innocent live or die.

Hence, unless and until good people are willing to train themselves to use their guns, without hesitation, for the purpose for which they were made, they are better off not possessing them. Their inhibition could translate into an opportunity for the uninhibited assailant to make his attack against them that much easier.

It *should* be, but apparently is not, obvious that none of this implies that a gun owner *must* always shoot to kill. No one, least of all me, is making or would ever make such an indiscriminate assertion. That being said, it is precisely the person who possesses both the skill and the will to kill an attacker that has the *choice*, based upon his own appraisal of the circumstances within which he finds himself, as to whether or not to take that course of action. The good guy trains to kill the bad guys so that *if* he should have to do so, he can.

It is *his* choice—not that of the savage (or savages) who preyed upon him.

The point of a martial art is one and the same as that of a gun. Given the extent to which martial arts in the contemporary Western world have been diluted, it's no surprise that this may come as a shock to many people (including, unfortunately, far too many practitioners of the martial arts), but "martial"—as in "*martial* art"—means "of or pertaining to war."

War.

Martial artists trained to critically injure, maim, and, ultimately, extinguish the being of their enemies on the battlefield.

This doesn't mean that the martial arts don't have spiritual, intellectual, ethical, aesthetic, and cultural significance. They most certainly do. Nor does it imply that there aren't health benefits to be reaped from training in the martial arts. There most certainly are. Rather, it is to simply underscore a brute fact that had always been taken for granted until this generation, due to a variety of reasons, proceeded to divest the "martial" from the *martial* arts: The martial arts exist first and most fundamentally to make their practitioners into peerless *killers*.

To repeat the point made above, any self-styled martial artist who so much as suggests otherwise should get out of the business, for whatever the art is in which he trains or trains others, it isn't a genuine *martial* art if it doesn't aim to accomplish this objective.

If this idea shocks the sensibilities of people who otherwise have no objections to the existence of militaries and police forces, then this proves that they've bought lock, stock, and barrel the Statist mentality of our times, the paradigm according to which only government agents can and should train in lethal violence for the sake of protecting innocents.

Private actors, in turn, must rely upon "the Experts," those same government agents, to safeguard them.

This mindset is not now, nor has it ever been, befitting a free people, as America's Founders knew as well as anyone who studied the subject. Nor is it manly. Women can and should train to be their own protectors, certainly, yet men, equipped, as they are, with far greater body strength than their female counterparts, are expected to be the principal protectors of those who are more vulnerable. Time permitting, it is all fine and good for a man to call the police in an emergency. It is another thing entirely for him to delegate all responsibility for the protection of himself and the women and children in his care to strangers wearing the badge of the State. In the last analysis, he must be prepared to defend his own, and at whatever cost, for a man is, and must train to recognize himself as being, the force that stands between, on the one hand, his loved ones, and, on the other, the criminals who would hurt them.

"But if I fight back, even in self-defense, *I* could be arrested!" This is the response that is most concerning, particularly given that it is made by people who *carry firearms*.

This fear of being arrested in the event that one has to get violent with the violent is another one of those mental blockages that could make the gun owner pause just long enough to give the bad guy enough time to kill him and his family. Besides this, though, it is idiotic when it is considered that the alternative to defending oneself and one's loved ones is to allow oneself and one's loved ones to be harmed or murdered! To choose not to defend oneself and those in one's care from the ravages of scumbags is to choose, in effect, to allow the scumbags the opportunity to inflict pain and death upon the innocent (including, potentially, one's children).

The only choice for a decent person to make in these circumstances is that of defeating the enemy by whatever means are necessary.

To paraphrase the old saying regarding charity, the protection of oneself and one's own begins at home.

ESSAY 29

The CATEGORICAL IMPERATIVES of the Warrior…and of Warrior Flow

WARRIOR FLOW HAS three unconditional commands by which its practitioners train to live.

The 18th century German philosopher Immanuel Kant distinguished conditional or *hypothetical* imperatives—"Close the door *if* you don't want to catch cold," "Study hard *if* you want to pass the class," "Don't be unjust to others *if* you want for them to trust you," etc.—from absolute or *categorical* imperatives— "Close the door;" "Study hard;" "Don't be unjust," and so forth.

Moral imperatives, Kant believed, are always categorical, for their binding character is not dependent upon any other considerations.

It's not: "Don't murder *if* you don't want to be arrested and sent off to prison; it's simply, *"Don't murder."*

Warrior Flow has three categorical imperatives:

1. LOGOS MAXIM: "KNOW REALITY."
2. ACTION MAXIM: "TRAIN TO KILL THE ENEMY."
3. VIRTUE MAXIM: "LIVE HONORABLY."

The **Logos** or **Knowledge Maxim** is the imperative to know how the universe actually works. It demands of students that they become familiar with the basic truths of both *physics* and human *physiology*.

Fighting, not unlike any and all other human activities, is constrained by the laws of the universe. Such laws include, of course, both the ways in which the human body operates as well as the ways in which human perception occurs. The drills for Warrior Flow are all intended to make a person more familiar with the truth of two fundamental axioms.

The first is what we may call the **Pan-Body Principle**:

> The human body is the human body and everyone's body moves **essentially** in the same ways.

The second is the Principle of Uniqueness:

> There are certain ways in which my body moves that are unique to my body.

Each principle rests upon the **Natural vs. *Normal* Thesis** (NNT). The latter, in turn, presupposes the *Teleological Postulate*. The Teleological Postulate is the same postulate endorsed by most pre-modern thinkers. The mechanical conception of the universe birthed by modern science and the concomitant decline in influence of more traditional and religious readings of the cosmos attended the separation in philosophy of the descriptive and the normative, of "facts" and "values," of the

163

"is" and the "ought."

Warrior Flow, however, is of one spirit with the ancient Greeks, ancient Romans, ancient Chinese, and the Jews and Christians from antiquity to the present in accepting the Teleological Postulate: If x *is* such-and-such a way, then it *ought* to be that way.

For example, if x is a knife, then since it is the very nature of a knife to cut, x ought to be able to cut.

Similarly, if the human body *naturally* moves in this or that way, then it *ought* to move in *this* or *that* way—and not in any others.

To be more to the point: No one, including and particularly practitioners of the martial arts, should condition their bodies to move *unnaturally*.

Given a lifetime of conditioning our bodies into a state of *forgetfulness*, of *alienation* from their natural state, their true selves, we have forgotten the effortlessness with which we once, long ago when we were children, maneuvered our way through the world.

For this reason, it has become normal, all too *normal*, for us to move our bodies as inefficiently.

But just because something has become the norm, means neither that it is natural nor that it is desirable. What it does mean, however, is that because it is an acquired set of circumstances, it can be mitigated and, with enough commitment, eradicated.

The **Action Maxim** demands of Warrior Flow students that they always train with an eye toward killing the enemy (the attackers of innocents, "the bad guys").

Notice, the imperative is *not* "Always *kill* the enemy." No one is in any position to dictate to a person who is in a potentially life-or-death situation the exact course of action that he should take. For whatever reasons, reasons that perhaps only a person in those circumstances at that moment can know, a person may decide to spare an attacker's life. Affirming, as it does, the free agency of the person, Warrior Flow honors its students' capacity to make choices.

However, Warrior Flow instructors will make sure that its students *can* choose. With an eye toward that end, they train them so that they can kill their attackers.

And this, in turn, means that those who pursue training in Warrior Flow must train so that they *will be able* to do just this.

The third imperative, the **Virtue Maxim**, is nothing more or less than the command that Warrior Flow students always and everywhere conduct themselves with honor. They are expected to bring honor to themselves, their loved ones, and their art.

Warrior Flow, being an art the ultimate justification of which is the equipping of decent people, from all backgrounds, with the ability to eliminate from the living any who would attack innocents, assumes that its practitioners will use their abilities to resolve only potentially life-or-death situations.

"Fights" of the proverbial schoolyard or barroom variety, besides being avoidable and prohibitively costly from a legal standpoint, are beneath the dignity of a warrior. Warriors don't "fight" in this sense of the term, in the sense of fighting to "beat someone's ass," say.

Warriors fight to neutralize the enemy by whichever means necessary. And the neutralization of the enemy could very well consist of maiming or killing him (or *them*).

For this reason, Warrior Flow students are peaceful. Yet they are as peaceful as was George Washington when he reminded his contemporaries and all future generations:

> *To be prepared for war is one of the most effectual means of preserving peace.*

ESSAY 30

Keeping Combat Impersonal

IN ORDER TO maximize a defender's chances for victory over an assailant, it is imperative that the defender avoid panic.

To mitigate panic, a self-defense student must train so as to be able to default to his or her training within a heartbeat. More specifically, the training should aim to accomplish the following things.

First, though the representatives of most contemporary martial arts systems insist that it is only by way of *gross* motor movement that a defender, under duress, can execute the techniques necessary to ward off an assailant, the truth of the matter is that proficiency in combat, like proficiency in any other activity, is achieved only at the level of *subtle* muscle control.

That is, it is only when the performance of a craft or activity becomes *second nature* to the practitioner, only when it has been trained to the subconscious level, that he or she can be said to have mastered it.

If targeted for attack, self-defense students whose training modality and methodologies aim to help them continually refine their movement so as to make it as efficient, as covert, as possible are not nearly as likely to panic as those who either aren't trained at all or whose training encourages wasteful motion (Training of this latter kind can transpire either, as in most classical martial arts and the "four pillars of MMA," when it is conducive to victory in a *sporting* match, as opposed to a life-or-death attack, or when it focuses on the overt implementation of techniques, of hand strikes and kicks, as is the case within the world of "Reality-based Self-Defense").

Second, panic can be avoided if self-defense students train to view the confrontation in terms of *war*.

The kind of encounter for which self-defense students are training, or should be training, has nothing to do with sport. Nor are self-defense students training to become law enforcement officers, whose job it is to subdue and arrest criminal suspects, or bouncers and security personnel who are hired to protect facilities from drunks and rabble-rousers of various types who imperil the safety of others.

Self-defense students are civilians who train only for the sake of protecting themselves and their loved ones from predators.

This means that they should be training to transform their minds, their *wills,* so as to become *warriors.*

More exactly, to reduce the likelihood that students of self-defense will panic when under attack, they must train to develop what, in Warrior Flow Combatives, is known as *"ruthless intention,"* the resolve to incapacitate the attacker (or attackers) by whatever means necessary. When students prepare themselves for, not the proverbial school yard fight or contest-centered confrontation, but all-out war, this has an impact on the psyche that is both sobering and liberating: It is sobering in that one knows precisely what needs and ought to be done in response to an attack, and it is liberating because this perfect clarity and moral certainty give rise to the will to reduce the predator to prey.

This unwavering commitment is freedom in that it endows a person with the power of choice, the choice to either crush an attacker into oblivion or, if circumstances allow it, to show just enough mercy to neutralize him while permitting him to live.

Third, it is, of course, true that when someone is trying to harm you, it's hard not take things personally. Still, martial students should labor rigorously to always frame their relationship to their attacker(s) in *impersonal* terms. The following considerations go some distance toward enabling them to do so.

1. In a literal sense, since most *attacks*, as opposed to so-called *"fights,"* transpire between strangers, the relationship between defender and assailant is indeed impersonal.

So, literally, there can be no personal feelings of animosity or hatred between defenders and assailants when they don't know each other.

2. Since the martial arts are the arts of war, martial arts or self-defense students must indeed remember that, fundamentally, they are training to become *warriors*. To this end, they must remind themselves that, just as the American military sets its sights on *"the* Enemy," so self-defense students must train with an eye toward vanquishing the Enemy—but never, *"my* enemy."

"My enemy" is personal.

3. Warriors must commit to never engage in the proverbial "shit-talking" that precedes many a violent confrontation. This last point may sound redundant given that this kind of posturing typically accompanies "social" violence that, transpiring as it does between people who know one another, is usually avoidable. Warriors, in contrast, train to use violence only when it

is the only alternative to innocents being injured or murdered and when, coming in the form of an attack by *a stranger* and seemingly from nowhere, is far less likely be signaled in advance by any trash-talk.

Nevertheless, what is typical is not absolute: Social violence could manifest itself in the form of an attack from which there is no retreating, and "anti-social" violence may involve its own share of shit-talking.

Still, shit-talking is unbefitting a warrior in training for several reasons, but among them is that it renders the relationship between a defender and an assailant all too *personal*. It's not a good mindset for the self-defense student to have.

The self-defense student, the warrior, takes nothing personally. All of those characteristics that individuate human beings from one another, attributes that are assigned meaning in any number of other social contexts (and that figure centrally in so-called "identify politics"), the warrior-in-training refuses to see. He trains so as to abstract them from the bodies to which they belong, for as far as he is concerned, all that is relevant is the body, or the bodies, that are moving to jeopardize innocents. But moving human bodies are bound by the same laws of physics that bind *all* bodies in motion, and all human bodies, from the biggest, fastest, and strongest, to the smallest, slowest, and weakest, are bound by the same laws of human physiology.

The warrior would no more think to participate in a shit-talking, dick-swinging, chest-thumping, eye-staring contest with a human being that is aggressively moving toward him than he would think to do the same with a grizzly bear, a cobra, a train, or any other entity dangerously heading his way.

No, for the warrior, the threat is nothing more or less than a moving body. And he knows, then, that the way to stop the threat is to stop the body's movement soon enough.

The warrior is the truest of egalitarians. *As a warrior* (and not in other respects), there isn't a trace of color-consciousness, ethnic chauvinism, classism, or religious bigotry in him: He is prepared to, if need be, injure, maim, and, kill *anybody* that moves toward him, or other innocents, in a threatening manner. He cares not a lick as to whether the predator in question is black or white, male or female, older or younger, religious or irreligious, rich or poor, Christian, Muslim, or Jew. The warrior has both the skill and the will to battle to the death, whether it's his own death or that of his attacker.

He is, however, indeed *prejudice.* The warrior is disposed, and is forever training himself to be disposed, toward assessing potential threats and nullifying them before they can materialize. He discriminates, but between bodies that are threatening and those that are not. Against those that are threatening he is predisposed to move with unrelenting violence if he must. As for those that pose no such threat, he wants only to co-exist with them in peace.

But it's never anything personal for the warrior.

ESSAY 31

The Enemy, not My Enemy: Setting the Mind for Victory in Battle

GIVEN THAT, BOTH literally and as a matter of historical fact, the *martial* arts are the arts of *war*, students of such arts train to destroy, as intelligently, creatively, and brutally as need be, *enemies*, as warriors on the battlefield have always squared off against enemies.

To put the point another way, there are no *opponents* on the battlefield. Sports contestants are opponents of one another. However, there is and can be no sportsmanship, no Marquis of Queensberry rules, in mortal combat.

Civilians who defend themselves against unprovoked physical assaults on the streets or in their homes are no different from soldiers in war: Civilians and soldiers are both immersed in violent confrontations that, devoid as they are of the numerous constraints within which athletes must operate to prevent them from seriously injuring themselves and their opponents, could easily result in death, whether that of the citizen or of those with whom the citizen is engaged.

Actually, civilians who must reckon with an attack upon being awakened in the middle of the night by home intruders, or who must defend themselves against bipedal predators who prey upon them while they're walking to their cars in a mall parking lot or while they're on a subway during an outing with their families in a large city, are in a more vulnerable position in many ways than is the soldier, for civilians, *unlike* soldiers, cannot rest comfortably knowing that they have the authority and the power of the State to do what needs to be done against those who have been identified by their own government as the Enemy. When a government is at war, the context for the violence that transpires is understood in advance by all involved. All of the players, so to speak, are reasonably known by and to one another, and the rules of engagement established.

Civilians, on the other hand, are in an entirely different sort of situation. The Enemy is among them, and can attack anywhere and at any time. While American citizens do have the Constitutional right to self-defense, nevertheless, and for good reason, lodged in the minds of the law-abiding is the fear that it is *they* who will be burdened with legal troubles for harming or killing the criminals who threaten them.

In other words, civilians, in contrast to soldiers, have this psychological adhesion with which to contend.

All of this being noted, it is the distinction between *the* Enemy and *my* enemy to which we need attend here. This is the distinction that it is crucial for the citizen who trains in self-defense to bear in mind.

It is conducive to the end of combat-readiness for self-defense students to think of those who would threaten themselves and other innocents as "enemies," for sure, but this is because the term "enemies" serves to distinguish combat training from sports training, where there are "opponents," as well as to forever remind students that they are to treat their training with all of the seriousness with which the military treats the training of its troops for war. Yet it's equally critical to think in terms of "*the* Enemy" as opposed to "*my* enemy."

The reason that doctors and nurses refer to their patients who died as having "expired," "termination of the pregnancy" and "abortion of the fetus" are used to describe the intentional killing of the ever-developing human being in its mother's womb, and "collateral damage" is used by the military to refer to innocent people who have been killed in war is the same reason for why those who train in a martial art should think of assailants as "the Enemy," rather than "my enemy": An individual who needs to defend himself against an assailant is likely to do so more adeptly if he views his attacker *impersonally*.

Those who wish to be victorious in battle need to at once *expand* their *psychological* or *emotional* distance from their attackers while *contracting* the *physical* distance separating them. Thinking of assailants as *the* Enemy serves this twofold purpose. Thinking of an attacker in terms of *my* enemy, though, is more likely to have just the opposite effect.

Hatred, anger, and fear are emotions that are not only unobjectionable considered in themselves. They are indispensable to victory in battle as long as, through training, the self-defense student has learned how to manage these passions so as to appropriate them productively when the time for doing so arises. These emotions, the self-defense student must never forget, already exist within him, for all human beings, and particularly human beings who have spent more than a little bit of time on Earth, know pain. We've all had our share of experiences that have caused us no small measure of hatred, of anger, of fear. In managing these emotions, the self-defense student learns how to utilize them constructively, as fuel for battle.

By thinking of an attacker as *the* Enemy, any personal connection that the defender may imagine exists between him and his attacker has been obviated, and the attacker is viewed for what he is, just an occasion for the defender to unleash what could be a lifetime's worth of the hatred, anger, and fear that is within him. Achieved is the psychological and emotional distance needed to prevent his anger and hatred from degenerating into blind rage, and his fear into panic.

At the same time, the defender—aware that the attacker, not being his own personal enemy, is a total stranger—will no longer be in danger of succumbing to the temptation to keep the attacker at a physical distance from himself, as one would be inclined to respond to an attack in the wild by recoiling from or trying to push oneself away from a predatory animal. By personalizing one's relationship with a *human* predator, by seeing him as *my* enemy, the person preyed upon risks wasting precious time and energy attempting to accomplish an impossible outcome: As attacks happen within the closest of ranges, up close and within the attacked person's sphere of influence, his "personal space," it is impossible for a defender to prevail over an attacker while busying himself with keeping the attacker at a distance.

But when an attacker is viewed impersonally, he can be regarded as simply one more body in motion that, as such, is subject to the same principles of physics to which all bodies are subject. In conceiving an attacker objectively and impartially as *the* Enemy, the attacker becomes nothing more and nothing less than a moving target, a material substance to be…*embraced.* Yes, by regarding an assailant impersonally, a defender's inclination will be to, not waste invaluable resources in time and energy trying to disengage from a predator who has already resolved to prey upon him but, rather, to embrace the predator by manipulating, subjugating, and dominating him as one would any other moving body that threatened one's life.

And the way to do *this* is to move *better* than the moving body that endangers one.

Moving better isn't necessarily to move *faster.* It is to move more *efficiently,* more *subtly,* i.e. with better *timing.*

To outmaneuver another body in motion is to cut off its movement before that movement becomes a problem.

The relationship between a bull and a matador makes the point. The matador would never think of regarding the bull as "my enemy." There is no bad blood between the two, no feelings of personal animosity of any sort on the part of the matador. As for the bull, on the other hand, the bull is enraged, and thinks of nothing else than gorging the matador to death. Now, the bull has every physical advantage over the matador: It is stronger, larger, faster, and, because of its rage, obviously more aggressive. Inasmuch, though, as the matador doesn't panic; insofar as he remains calm and collected, he is able to neutralize all of the bull's physical strengths by getting ahead of the bull's movement, by moving with such subtlety, with such precision, that the bull doesn't realize where the matador is until it is too late.

Had the matador moved too soon, he wouldn't have stood a chance against the bull. And had he moved too late, he clearly would've been killed. But as long as he moves at just the right moment, and as little as he can, he wins.

The matador views the bull as matter in motion. Period. He knows that regardless of how fast and large that body is, it can be defeated as long he can get ahead of it, as long as he can time his own movement so as to re-situate himself at a future spatial and temporal location where he anticipates he'll need to be and from which he'll be able to prevail over the bull.

"The Enemy," to reiterate, is indeed an apt name for the wicked who prey upon innocents, for anyone who seeks to inflict harm and death upon innocents is nothing if not the enemy of God and humanity, of the Good, the True, and the Beautiful.

But in order for the decent to maximize their odds of being able to prevail over evil doers, they should try to avoid personalizing their relationship to them. The Enemy is a moving body, a body, mind you, that, being finite and composed of matter, is bound by the same laws of physics that bind all bodies, and the same principles of human physiology that constrain all human beings. Whatever the natural talents and physical attributes of an assailant, and whatever weapons he may have on

175

him, if his would-be victim moves *first* so as to preempt the assailant from doing the things with his body that he needs to do in order to successfully execute his attack, it matters not what physical disadvantages the defender is at, he wins—as long as, of course, he exploits the microseconds that the Enemy wastes being discombobulated by becoming the attacker himself, by going on offense, thus depriving the Enemy of even more time as the defender gains it.

ESSAY 32

Rory Miller's *Meditations on Violence: A Comparison of Martial Arts Training & Real World Violence*: A Review

RORY MILLER'S BOOK was published quite some time ago. Still, precisely because it has deservedly achieved something like the status of a minor classic amongst martial artists, it continues to invite dialogue.

In lucid, engaging prose, Miller, a lifelong martial artist and now retired corrections officer (who also spent some time in the military and as a bouncer), draws upon decades-worth of his personal encounters with violent actors in reflecting on the nature of violence itself.

And while he concedes from the outset that he doesn't presume to supply an exhaustive account of violence, that the author *aspires* to provide as comprehensive a taxonomy of violence as any that has heretofore been available is demonstrably the case. Whether Miller succeeded in realizing this ambition, this can't be said for certain. What *is* certain, though, is that the goal is valuable and Miller, who made as good a go in its pursuit as anyone, is to be commended for his efforts.

At a little more than 200 pages, *Meditations* is not a particularly long book. Neither, however, is it particularly short. Its length, rather, is exactly what a reader, whether someone from within the martial arts/self-defense industry or a lay person who may just be interested in learning more about violence, would expect from a work whose every syllable is utilized with maximal efficiency to make the articulation of its author's wide-reaching thoughts on the subject matter both cogent and—what's even more impressive—compelling. To be sure, Miller's virtues as a writer are many. The explicitness of the content of *Meditations* as well as the organization of its presentation are peerless.

Still, while it is with all of the justification in the world that Miller has reaped the praise for his *Meditations* that has been visited upon it, there are some concerns that need to be addressed.

Miller's experience dealing with violent, dangerous people is extensive and rich. Of this there can be no doubt. He has much grist for the mill that is his meditations on violence, indeed. However, the vast majority of Miller's violent encounters transpired while he was on the job. He freely and repeatedly acknowledges this. Interestingly, though, while spending a portion of his book identifying the potential drawbacks of various training methodologies (including, to his credit, the training methods that he himself appropriated), Miller does not, from what I could find, claim to recognize that the *context* within which much of his experience with violence occurred could itself be a limitation when it comes to teaching *civilians.*

It's not just that, generally speaking, most LEOs and soldiers are relatively young, reasonably fit males (who, as such, have a measure of natural strength and athleticism that make it easier for them to administer whatever use of force they're permitted to use for the purposes specific to their professions). Corrections officers—like law enforcement personnel generally and military personnel as well—operate under conditions that are of a fundamentally different kind than those in which civilians find themselves. LEOs and soldiers are *agents of the State* that, as such, are usually *identifiable by some means* (like a uniform of some kind, say, or a badge). They are *authorized* to employ force, *within limits*, against those—like enemy combatants, criminal suspects, and convicts—whom the State has, for reasons peculiar to the relevant context(s)—like war, public safety, and maintaining order within penal institutions—deemed fit for its application.

As Al, who, it bears repeating here, is a retired Marine Corps Lieutenant-Colonel and veteran of multiple tours of combat in Iraq and Afghanistan, repeatedly reminds his students, he, like every other service person deployed to the Middle East, was there for a distinct mission. They were readily identifiable and equipped with weaponry of various sorts that enabled them to execute that mission.

So too is Rory Miller's circumstance of being a corrections officer similar to that a soldier in a warzone in that he too knew who the bad guys were, as they knew him. And he knew *where* they were. Miller had ample resources, including, as a sergeant, a team of officers under his command, with which to address whatever violence might erupt.

What's true of Al's situation as a combat soldier in wartime and that of Miller's as a corrections officer is, of course, equally true of the situation of a police officer.

The point of all of this is that a civilian in her home who finds herself awakened at 3:00 AM by armed intruders, or who is set upon by bipedal vermin while making her way through the mall parking lot to her car, is in a radically different set of circumstances than those in which LEOs and soldiers are situated.

This is obvious.

Yet it's an instance of the obvious that needs to be stated—particularly to those within the martial arts/self-defense industry.

This isn't to suggest that a martial arts instructor whose background is in law enforcement and who teaches civilians is necessarily unaware of these crucial, and crucially dramatic, contextual differences. Nor is it to imply that he isn't competent to teach civilians how to win the fight for their lives. The intention here, rather, is to register two observations:

1) This *is* a difference of which, if their *silence on the matter* is any indication, few martial artists *appear* aware.

2) Miller's is a book—to be sure (in case I wasn't clear above), a high-quality one at that—on the nature, types, causes, and principles of *violence*, a work in which the author seems to relish in not just puncturing the delusions, myths, and fantasies that are endemic in the universe that is the contemporary world of the martial arts, but accentuating as well the shortcomings in *all* training methodologies.

He may or may not have intended it, but it's nearly impossible to escape the impression that Miller is, what we may call, a martial *skeptic* (of which more will be said below). One would think, then, that he would note that the nature of much of his experience with violence, as brutal and dangerous as it was, and while it could only be an asset in teaching other LEOs, *could* be a *liability* if it is the lens through which he supplies instruction to civilians.

To put it simply, corrections officers have an obligation to subdue unruly prisoners. Law-abiding citizens who only want to live and let live are under no such obligation to subdue a would-be rapist or any other type of violent thug who means to do harm to them and their loved ones.

The training tactics taught to one group need to be different in kind from those imparted to another. As long as an instructor has the ability to speak these two tongues, as it were, and the perceptiveness to know the proper occasions for speaking both, there isn't a problem. Miller has a solid reputation. It is not our intention to question his competence on this score. Still, the distinction should be observed.

From our reading of *Meditations,* Miller, who is, demonstrably, the tireless martial skeptic, somehow fails to take note of it.

The contemporary martial arts arena being what it is, the value of a skeptical eye can't be overstated.

That being said, *being skeptical* and *skepticism* are two entirely different things.

The first is a lively, healthy disposition. The other is what occurs when that disposition is abstracted from the other character traits with which it coexists and by which it's qualified and transformed into a *dogma,* an *ideology,* or a *creed.* The dogmatist whose dogma is skepticism is no less a true believer in *his* dogma than is the martial artist who he criticizes a believer in his. Because the dogmatic skeptic rejects all other martial arts systems *a priori,* as it were, he has none of the appreciation for nuance, the discernment and discrimination, possessed by the skeptic that isn't a dogmatist.

We don't mean to imply that Miller actually is a dogmatic skeptic. Quite the contrary, for as we've been at pains to stress, *Meditations* is a remarkably thoughtful work. Still, while we would disagree that Miller *is* a dogmatic skeptic, there are times when he *sounds* like one, like unless he is aware of the distinction between being skeptical and skepticism, his otherwise insightful commentary runs the risk of being mistaken for but one more species of run-of-the-mill contrarianism.

There's nothing run-of-the-mill about Rory Miller's *Meditations on Violence: A Comparison of Martial Arts Training & Real World Violence.*

We just urge its author to be mindful of the temptation to turn one's critique of the creeds of *bullshido masters* into but another creed.

www.ingramcontent.com/pod-product-compliance
Lightning Source LLC
Chambersburg PA
CBHW021402090426
42742CB00009B/965